POWER NOW

You are powerful.

Kristin Bhaqat

POWER NOW

THE ART OF GETTING WHAT YOU WANT

HOW TO MASTER YOUR MIND & LOVE YOUR LIFE

Kirsten Bloomquist

Power Now

Copyright © 2019 by Kirsten Bloomquist

All rights reserved. No part of this publication may be reproduced, distributed, or transmitted in any form or by any means, whatsoever, including photocopying, recording, storing in a retrieval system, or other electronic or mechanical methods, without the prior written, signed and dated permission of the author, except in the case of brief quotations embodied in critical reviews and certain other non-commercial uses permitted by copyright law. For permission, email your request, addressed "Attention: Permission Request," at the address below.

feelingpowerfulnow@gmail.com

www.feelingpowerful.com

Ordering Information: Quantity sales: Special discounts are available on quantity purchases by corporations, associations, and others. For details, email the address above, addressed, "Attention: Bulk Order Request."

Special Edition Prints: If your corporation or business sees it beneficial to print a special edition of this book for business and branding purposes, please contact the address above.

Orders by trade bookstores and wholesalers: Please contact the address above.

ISBN 978-1-9990911-0-1

Printed in Vancouver, British Columbia, Canada

Limits of Liability/Disclaimer of Warranty

The author and publisher of this book have used their best efforts in preparing this material. The author and publisher disclaim any warranties (expressed or implied), or merchantability for any particular purpose. The author and publisher shall in no event be liable for any loss or other damages, including, but not limited to special, incidental, consequential, or other damages. The information presented in this publication is compiled from sources believed to be accurate at the time of printing, however, the publisher and author assumes no responsibility for errors or omissions. The information in this publication is not intended to replace or substitute professional advice. The author and publisher specifically disclaim any liability, loss, or risk that is incurred as a consequence, directly or indirectly, of the use and application of any of the contents or this information. The author and publisher bear no responsibility for the accuracy of the information on any websites cited and/or used by the author in this book.

Acclaim for *Power Now:*

"*This is the book I have been looking for! Power Now* sets the stage for incorporating robust mental tools that will allow for lasting happiness and success. I highly recommend this book to anyone who is struggling with self-doubt and self-sabotage, or anyone wanting to lead a purpose-driven life. Well done, Kirsten."

Todd Judkins, Author, Podcast Host, Performance Coach

"This book is a go-to when going through tough times. Read this profoundly inspirational book and you will equip yourself with the mental strengths, skills and tools to overcome just about anything and unleash your full potential. Kirsten echoes that you have the power to redesign your life, to master your life and to get what you want. You will find your joy and magic even in the darkest moments and in periods of disappointments and frustrations."

Juliet "Jhet" Torcelino van Ruyven, Amazon Best Selling Author, Speaker, Mentor and World Traveller. Co-Founder: www.FeelingPowerfulAcademy.com

"Ever wonder why someone seems to have the perfect life? *Power Now* is the toolbox that provides the skills to develop and maintain the perfect life for you. Kirsten lays out the theoretical knowledge about how our inner self and outside world is connected. She also provides real-life examples and actionable items for anyone to gain control of the mind. For anyone who's either looking to achieve their ultimate goal in life, or maintain a topnotch state at all times, this book is the perfect read."

Holmes Wang, Wealth Advisor

"*Power Now* is a deep dive into the inner workings of our subconscious mind. You will learn powerful techniques that are incredibly simple and easy to utilize. These techniques have the ability to release you from old patterns and hidden beliefs that have been holding you back. Kirsten shares real life experiences that are easy to relate and easy to understand. Grab two copies- One for yourself and one for someone you love!"

Amy Donaldson, Speaker, Coach, Author of *Get Off the Cash Flow Roller Coaster*

"This book is a pocketbook of knowledge that changed my life."

Sian Combrink

"Kirsten is remarkable! *Power Now* truly helps readers to understand the mind and equips them with coping skills to navigate life. This is a must read!"

Jessica Jillings, Photographer

"She tells you how to program your mind to get the life that you want, too. I highly recommend buying this book- it's fantastic!"

Ann Beaudet, Author, Blogger, Speaker Educator

"I highly recommend this book. It explains the power of the mind while giving practical, real-world advice that anyone can use. If you are looking to improve any aspect of your life, whether it be health, wealth, relationships, self-confidence - you name it - read and re-read this book and take action. You will be well pleased with the results."

Maryam Ferdosian, Naturopathic Doctor at East Van Integrated Health Clinic, Author

Dedication

To Raf,
I have everything I want
with you.

Power Now

Table of Contents

WHAT THIS BOOK IS ABOUT	1
INTRODUCTION	4
CHAPTER 1: MY SECRET FORMULA	7
PILLAR 1: CONNECT	*10*
CHAPTER 2: CONNECT TO YOUR SUBCONSCIOUS MIND	11
CHAPTER 3: COMMAND YOUR POWER	22
CHAPTER 4: THE ULTIMATE MIND HACK	28
CHAPTER 5: HYPNOTIZE YOURSELF	44
CHAPTER 6: CONNECT TO WHAT YOU WANT	57
PILLAR 2: CLEAR	*62*
CHAPTER 7: WHAT THE FORK?	63
CHAPTER 8: CLEAR LIMITING PAST PROGRAMMING	66
CHAPTER 9: CLEAR CURRENT NEGATIVE CONDITIONING	76
CHAPTER 10: SHIFT MENTAL PATTERNS	85
CHAPTER 11: EMOTIONS	90
CHAPTER 12: BOOST YOUR MOTIVATION	97
PILLAR 3: CREATE	*102*
CHAPTER 13: LIFE IS LIKE A GAME OF POKER	103
CHAPTER 14: CREATE A NEW INTERNAL BELIEF SYSTEM	107
CHAPTER 15: CREATE A NEW REALITY	113
CHAPTER 16: CREATE TRIGGERS AND BUTTONS	119
CHAPTER 17: THE ART OF ASKING FOR WHAT YOU WANT	122
CHAPTER 18: OWN YOUR POWER	130
BONUS CHAPTER: EXPERTS' SUCCESS STORIES	137
CONCLUSION: YOUR SUCCESS	155
ACKNOWLEDGEMENTS	162
REFERENCES	163

Power Now

What This Book Is About

You picked up this book for a reason. Whatever drew you to these pages, I am happy you are here, and I appreciate you putting your trust in me and allowing me to be your "coach" throughout this journey of discovering and maximizing your inner potential.

My training as a Clinical Hypnotherapist and Master Hypnotist has led me to understand how to get results by using the power of the subconscious mind. I help people to reprogram their subconscious minds to overcome limiting beliefs and get what they want.

Do you wonder if you have more potential within you, and that it may be wasting away because you have never learned how to fully access it and apply it? Do you know deep down that you are destined for greater things? Do you sometimes feel like there are invisible barriers holding you back, and the harder you try, the more resistance you face?

I have good news and bad news for you. The bad news is your mind has already been programmed and a lot of that programming is detrimental to you and your dreams.

The good news is your subconscious mind can successfully be reprogrammed at any age or time. You do not even need to be at your prime for this to happen. In fact, I was able to completely transform my mind while I was at my lowest.

Even if you feel stuck, lost, overwhelmed and experience self-doubt right now, you can break free from those chains, and program your subconscious mind to start living your happiest and most fulfilled life.

Would you like to be able to reprogram your mind to be more confident, victorious, happy, creative, bold, fulfilled and successful? Would you enjoy being able to command your mind and direct its power towards reaching your goals? Would you like to use the fastest methods to give yourself an elite edge?

Before we get started, I want to take a moment to inform you what this book is about, what it is not about, and how it is different from the other books out there.

This book is NOT about me repackaging cliché phrases like, "Just think positive!" or "Believe in yourself!" However, this book will give you techniques to overcome the inner doubts that are weighing you down and help you to develop an asset superior to self-confidence: self-certainty. When you have self-confidence, you *feel* well. When you have self-certainty, you *do* well.

This book is NOT about doing anything unethical, such as violating consent or using forceful methods. In fact, this book has nothing to do with controlling others. However, it will teach you simple and effective techniques to control your own mind and program it to achieve your desires.

The strategies in this book are timeless. These skills will not become outdated in the future. They are skills that you can use for the rest of your life, in any situation- both good and bad.

The strategies in this book can be applied to any goal you have in mind. There is no need to learn an entirely new process each time you set a new goal. This book is like having the manual for your subconscious mind. Learn the principles and apply them to all the different areas of your life.

Everything taught within this book is knowledge and strategies that I continually use and practice, both with my clients and myself.

Throughout my career I have had the honor of serving entrepreneurs, professional athletes, celebrity figures, doctors, CEO's, business teams and even a billionaire. This book contains the same strategies I taught them.

Plus, I interviewed a few aspirational experts for this book, and they shared their top methods to creating both a successful mind and life. A few of these remarkable people include: a former panelist on the T.V. show Dragons' Den; the poker player who won the most amount of money of all time in one year; and a professional dancer who holds many titles, including five-time world champion.

In addition, I had the honor and advantage of having a wise, witty and wonderful man, by the name of Mike Cantrell, contribute his best business building strategies (over 45 years of expertise), all simmered down into simple actionable steps that get superb results. If you are going to create what you want, you are going to have to know what you want, how to ask for it and how to close the deal- and he is the exact guy to learn from, as he has successfully closed several lucrative deals, funding campaigns for high ranking politicians in the past.

The knowledge I am revealing in this book has been kept as simple and as straightforward as possible. The easier a specific strategy appears to you, the more likely you will be to use it daily to quickly generate the results you want.

Are you ready to finally gain control and become the master of your mind? When you master your mind, you master yourself.

Self-Mastery = Life Mastery.

Introduction

Hitting Rock Bottom

It was past midnight and I was lying on my bedroom floor, with tears gushing down my face. A few months before, I had lost the closest person to me to cancer and it devastated me, to say the least.

I had done everything I could to keep myself together, and to build momentum to move myself forward, but, the harder I tried, the more things seemed to go wrong. My dreams were disintegrating into sand, slipping between my fingers and out of my hands completely.

I felt like I was having an out – of – body experience, watching myself spiral downwards into a dark vortex. It appeared as though I was going deeper and deeper, faster and faster and I had no clue as to what was up or down, anymore. I was overwhelmed with feelings of being lost, alone and afraid. And I didn't know who I was, anymore.

This was not where I wanted to be. I knew I should be doing better ... and that I *could* be doing better. I was weak and exhausted. What made things worse was that I was still putting everyone else first out of habit and I had no energy left for myself. Things needed to change – and quickly.

That night, on my bedroom floor, in a puddle of my own tears, I said a small prayer, out of sheer desperation, "God, Universe, higher self ... I let go. I surrender. I need help. I know I can become better and stronger for having gone through these challenges. Please help me to get through this. I am ready for happiness and great things to start happening. What do I do next? Please show me..."

Power Now

After waiting a few moments in silence, and having zero answers come to mind, I slowly picked myself up off the floor and pulled myself into bed. I went to sleep with one thought on my mind: "I will get through this and become even better *because* of this time. There has to be a way…"

The next day I got my answer – I had an "aha" moment and a knowingness filled my mind.

The only way *out* of this madness was *through* it. I came to the conclusion that I might as well stop fearing the messiness and craziness of breaking down and I told myself to become fully present to the entire experience, instead. This phase would come to an end soon enough, and it would be the catalyst which would recreate my entire life.

I had no clue *how* that would happen… I just knew that it *would* happen. I felt assured that I would be pushed to greater things and truly be able to enjoy them *because* I had been through this challenge. I asked myself, "What can I learn from this experience? What is it here to teach me? How can I become better *because* of this?"

I decided to stop trying to do everything on my own, and get the right team in place to empower me towards my goals. That was one of the best decisions I ever made. The guidance was the uplifting breakthrough that I needed in order to heal, turn myself around and find my way, again. That dreadful phase of my life taught me to train my mind to always, always find the silver lining.

What was the silver lining in hitting rock bottom? There were a few hidden blessings. Hitting rock bottom inspired me to switch both my gears and my focus. I slowed down and concentrated on healing and satisfying my soul by spending my time doing the things that mattered most to me.

Losing everything caused me to start over from ground zero, which is where I discovered a secret formula that gave me the ability to recreate myself the way I wanted to be and to set myself in a new and thrilling direction. And now, I can proudly say my soul feels alive and fulfilled.

Plus, there were several other unexpected benefits of my secret formula. I discovered how to get into alignment with my highest self. I became able to clear away negative thought patterns and behaviours, and create habits for success (these actions became automatic and unconscious, working for me without much conscious attention). I gained the ability to program myself with a "Happiness Button," which works on command.

And, my favorite of all, I have attained the skills to come out on top of challenging situations- as if they were rigged in my favor from the beginning. Can you imagine what a game-changer that would be if you could live your life that way, too?

These dramatic changes did not happen overnight for me- it took me seven years to discover this formula. However, since I found this formula, I have applied it every time I came across a new problem and needed to create change. Not only does it work, but the process has been expedited, sometimes producing results in a matter of days or weeks. If I told you some results happen within hours, you probably would not believe me...

However, if I could overcome all of those challenges and produce results, then, you can, too. Things can turn around quickly for you, too. Are you starting to see that? It is O.K. to not have all the answers. It is O.K. to feel lost sometimes. The key is in knowing how and when to pull yourself together again, so that you can make the most out of yourself and get the most out of your life. The journey inwards is not the easiest one; however, it is the best and most rewarding journey of a lifetime. Are you starting to get excited about accomplishing your desires and feeling fulfillment deep within your soul?

It is sad to think of how many people die with the regret of not pursuing their dreams and passions. But, what is worse is how many people are living with those same regrets- that is like feeling their soul die a little more each day. Prevent that from happening to you. Now is the time to make a change and do something to satisfy your soul. Perhaps, *Power Now* can awaken your soul and spark the fulfillment you desire.

Are you ready for my secret formula?

Chapter 1
My Secret Formula

How to Program Your Mind to Achieve Just About Anything

My secret formula consists of three pillars, which I also refer to as, the 3 Pillars of Reprogramming Your Mind to Get What You Want.

You see, at first, I felt lost and broken. I was unhappy and felt like I had no control. Then I incorporated this three pillar formula into my life and now I feel happy, free and powerful.

These are the same three pillars I use when a person hires me to work with them one-on-one. If you want to get the best results, then apply these strategies, as if I am coaching you one-on-one. All three pillars are necessary in order to create a breakthrough, replace past mental programming that is holding you back and to reprogram your mind to create the life you desire.

If one pillar is missing, or simply overlooked, the subconscious mind may revert back to its old patterns. You are reading this because you are seeking lasting change, am I correct? Please avoid skipping ahead. Make sure you read this book in order and refer back to it often.

I will walk you through the pillars and show you how to make them work for you. Your best life is awaiting you.

Diagram 1: The 3 Pillars of Reprogramming Your Mind to get What You Want.

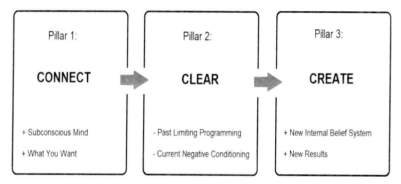

Power Now will dive into the three pillars of reprogramming your mind, and put them into bite size chunks, while providing you with effective methods that you can use from the comfort of your own home. You can start to master your mind and create the life you love- today!

Getting Started: Stop Where You Are

You are here because you want results. There are two things you must address first to get the best results. Get out a journal and a pen, open a notepad on your phone, or write an email to yourself. Results start after you become clear and write down the answers to the following two steps:

1. Document where you currently are. Take note of these things and be honest with yourself:

    a.) On a scale of 1-10, where are you in terms of reaching your goals? 1= far away from your goals, 10= you have already reached them.

    b.) On a scale of 1-10, how do you feel about the life you are living? 1= unhappy, 10= you are living your best life.

    c.) How do you generally feel about yourself on a daily basis? List any emotions or thought patterns that you frequently experience.

    d.) On a scale of 1-10, how do you feel about your ability to control your mind? 1= you have no control, 10= you can control it well.

e.) How much time do you spend taking care of your mind each day? Include meditation, visualization, therapy, reading, etc.

f.) Document the details of where you are starting from. Take a picture of yourself, take note of your stress level, your job situation, your relationship satisfaction and anything else that is important to you. This is your starting point. It is necessary to know these things in order to document your success.

2. Document where you want to be.

One of the best pieces of advice, from a hugely successful businessman, and former panelist on the TV show, Dragon's Den, W. Brett Wilson says to start by defining what success means to you. Challenge the definition. To one person, success might mean earning one million dollars per year. To another person, success could mean becoming personally enlightened and living each day filled with joy. Know what you want.

a.) What does success mean to you? Define it and lay it out. What does success feel like and look like?

b.) What will it feel like to have control of your mind- How will you know when you have done so?

c.) What other goals would you like to achieve? Include a mix of both physical and mental/emotional/spiritual goals. Do you want more happiness, confidence, fulfillment, inner peace, enlightenment, calmness, coping skills, etc.?

d.) What will it look like to have attained those dreams- how will you know when you have reached your goal?

e.) Why do you want to reach your goals? What is motivating you to get there?

f.) Why do you want to reach your goals now?

g.) What will you do to celebrate when you have reached your goals?

Keep your answers in a safe and handy place where you will remember them. It is important to be able to measure your results and document your progress, which we will do later in this book.

PILLAR 1

CONNECT

Chapter 2
Connect to Your Subconscious Mind

The Benefits of Pillar 1: Connect
- Get clear on what you want
- Gain focus
- Increase calmness and relaxation, physically and mentally
- Learn how to get "in the zone" on command
- Switch your mind to a creative and productive state
- Be present in the moment
- Heighten self-awareness
- Increase overall well-being, happiness and positivity
- Add balance into your day
- Access your internal power and discover your inner potential
- Get out of survive mode and enter thrive mode

What Will You Be Connecting to?

In my early twenties I was extremely closed-minded and skeptical. I was given a book about the power of the subconscious mind. I read through it from cover to cover and thought…

That is a load of BS!

I did not believe we had the ability to alter our destiny or fix ourselves.

Now, here I am with my own book about the power of the mind. And I can tell you, you have ultimate power and potential within you- enough to change your life, accomplish your dreams and create the life you want.

When I speak about the word "power" throughout this book, I am not talking about using unethical manipulation techniques, crooked psychological tactics, force or dominance to control people. Those are a false sense of power.

True power is the life force within you enabling you to gain control over yourself, attain your goals and design the life you really want. Power is not something you have; it is something you already are, something you tune into.

You will be learning several effective methods to tune in to two mighty forces:

1. Your subconscious mind (some may refer to it as your higher self, your internal guidance system, your intuition or your unconscious mind). Your subconscious is the essence of who you are.

2. Your goals (dreams, desires: what you want). Having big goals and connecting to what you want will flood your life with purpose. When your purpose is strong and ignites you from within, it will power you through just about anything.

Before I teach you effective techniques to tap into your potential, you must first know about the mind.

What is the Mind?

Some monks have been known to use their minds to slow their heartbeat right down to zero, be pronounced dead, and then command their heart to start back up at a predetermined time a couple of days later. While that is obviously not recommended for most people, it proves the extreme potential of our capabilities.

People have used this same energy to help themselves heal, create world-transforming inventions, make millions of dollars, completely change their lives, and achieve their wildest dreams. In dire circumstances, human beings have been known to lift cars to save somebody trapped underneath. This capability exists within every one of us, including you.

There are three main parts of the mind: the conscious mind, the critical faculty and the subconscious mind. We will mainly be focussing on the conscious and subconscious mind.

The conscious part is said to be roughly 5% of the mind and is your logical, analytical, thinking mind. This is the part of the mind you use to set goals, such as taking your business or career to the next level or getting into better physical shape. The conscious mind likes to think it knows everything.

The critical faculty is the gatekeeper to your subconscious mind.

The subconscious mind is the other (approximately) 95% of the mind and contains your memories and programming, attributing to your characteristics, fears and talents. This is the emotional/feeling part of your mind. It will largely influence whether you reach your goals or not, depending upon your programming. Your subconscious was molded between birth and the age of 7 by the main authority figures present at that time (usually your parents, family members and teachers), the events that happened to you, and how you *interpreted* those events.

The main function of the subconscious mind is to help you survive, which means helping you to feel comfortable and secure. This part of the mind sticks to what is familiar, such as patterns, some of which may not necessarily be in your best interest.

The bad news is that truly changing your mind takes time (the amount of time varies for everyone). The good news is, changing your *mindset* is instantaneous. And the best news is, the quickest way to redesign your mind is through your ability to switch your mindset. When you can control your state, you are the one holding the keys to your source of power and, ultimately, your destiny.

Diagram 2: The Mind

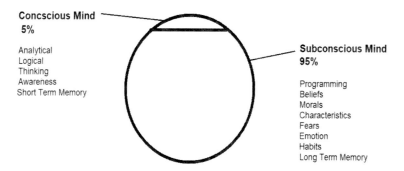

The Laws of the Mind

The Earth works by Natural Law. These are forces which are unbiased, unchangeable, omnipresent, available to all, and unseen, except for the effects they cause. For example: gravity. Though you cannot see it, gravity is always operating; it cannot be stopped or prevented, yet you can see its effects. It does not matter if a person who is rich or poor, young or old, big or small jumps off a cliff, gravity works the same for everybody. By learning how it works, we can work with it and "defy" it. For example, by flying in an airplane.

An important Law to acknowledge is that of Cause and Effect. This law is the most dominant of all, permeating the world and everything in it. It is commonly stated as, "You reap what you sow." A garden does not care whether the gardener sows' poisonous plants or strawberries. The Law of Cause and Effect applies no matter what. If fruit is planted, the garden yields fruit. If weeds are planted, weeds will result. The garden does the same amount of work. Even if the gardener intended to plant fruit, but planted weeds instead, this law ensures the harvest is determined by the seeds.

What does the Law of Cause and Effect have to do with your mind? It *is* your mind. Your conscious mind is the cause and your subconscious mind is the effect. Thoughts are a cause. Emotions and feelings are an effect. Dwelling on those thoughts, emotions and feelings (cause) = creating more of those thoughts, emotions and feelings (effect).

However, your feelings and surroundings can also cause specific thoughts. A happy mood can help ideas and creativity to flow through your mind, while stress can trigger negative thoughts that sometimes feel like they are stuck on repeat.

Being that the subconscious is programmed by the past (cause), it will often continue repeating the past (effect), until it is reprogrammed. Gravity and electricity are similar to the mind: you cannot see them, you can only see their effects.

Do Thoughts Contain Enough Power to Change Your Body?

While I was giving a lecture to a room full of medical doctors and oncologists, teaching them about the power of the subconscious, there was one demonstration that got them jumping out of their seats with excitement. I showed them how their thoughts can trigger the brain to create chemical reactions within the body. I am sharing it with you here. Please follow along to the best of your ability in order to experience the desired results:

Imagine yourself in your kitchen at home, walking over to your refrigerator and opening the door. On the top shelf is a bright, yellow lemon. Picture yourself reaching in and grabbing it. Maybe you can imagine the cold bumpy rind of the lemon against your fingertips. See yourself closing the fridge door and walking over to the counter where you slice your fruits and vegetables. A sharp knife lies on the cutting board. In your mind's eye, see yourself slicing a wedge out of the lemon, taking the wedge and bringing it close to your nose. Can you imagine the crisp, tart smell of the lemon? Now, I would like you to imagine taking a big, juicy bite out of the lemon's flesh. Perhaps the tangy juice causes your cheeks to pucker. Perhaps your mouth starts to water, too. Now go ahead and swallow the lemon juice.

Did you start to salivate? For most people, the answer is yes. This is because your subconscious mind does NOT know the difference between reality and imagination. Therefore, by placing your focus on the lemon, using your imagination, you were able to convince your mind you were eating a lemon. Your brain triggered a chemical reaction, which is the start of your digestive process: salivation.

Feel free to do that demonstration again and experience it profoundly, as I guide you through it in a video you will find at www.feelingpowerful.com/resources.

Can Thoughts Affect Your Health?

"You can't change your DNA but you can change the way your DNA code is expressed (your epigenetics)," says Dr. Lois Nahirney, the owner of the company, DNA Power, which specializes in DNA and epigenetics. "DNA expresses itself differently depending upon attitude, health, sleep, diet, toxins, etc."

"Your genes do switch on and off," Dr. Nahirney observes. "If you have mutated genes, your body tends to switch that way over time. If you have a healthy lifestyle, it can prevent that switch." That is great news, right? Are you wondering how you do that?

Dr. Nahirney continues, "Even if you inherit genes that make you prone to autoimmune or other diseases, really great diet and health and attitude can make a difference. You may have a predisposition, but a healthy lifestyle can help. We've seen that in cancers; that people with a very positive, 'can do attitude' will live longer.

"Positive mindset and energy are a huge part of switching on or off our genetics," she says. You have the opportunity to change your mind-set at any time and by doing so, you are switching more than just your attitude… you are making changes to your mental programming *and* your physical programming.

"Power is owning who you are and being comfortable and confident. Love is the answer. Find your uniqueness and let it shine." Dr. Nahirney.

As you may now understand, your thoughts trigger feelings and chemical responses within your body. Here are a few more examples of ways in which your thoughts create measurable reactions within your body:

Thinking about and Focussing on (Cause):	Chemical/Physical Reaction (Effect):
Winning the Lottery	Feelings of excitement, thrill, adventure, energy and happiness. Quickening heart rate, smiling and daydreaming.
Stressful situations Example: work or your to-do list	Feelings of stress, worry and anxiety. Tightness in the pit of your stomach, jitters, restlessness, excessive sweating, heart beat speeding up, etc.
Things you fear Example: standing at the edge of a tall building	Feelings of dizziness, vertigo, panic, fear. Sweaty hands, butterflies in the stomach, jitters, heart beat speeding up, muscles tightening, etc.
Your happiest memory	Feelings of happiness, joy, calmness. Smiling, breathing slowing down, muscles relaxing, etc.
Your favorite meal	Feelings of excitement, happiness and hunger. Growling stomach and salivation.
Someone you find sexually attractive	Physical arousal

What Do You Think?

You are not your thoughts. You are the observer of your thoughts. Thoughts can become powerless when you learn to observe them from a state of detachment. This takes practice. Just because you believe in something, does not mean it is true. That being said, thoughts contain a whole lot of power and potential, especially when you believe them, repeat them or think them with strong enough emotion.

Power Now

Believing firmly in something will have some sort of an effect on you or your lifestyle. For instance, if you believe it is too dangerous to drive your car, you may develop a fear of driving, which can lead to a phobia that prevents you from driving altogether. When this happens, it is because the belief is so real, irrational thoughts become the reality within your mind, altering your feelings and behaviours.

Most people are so caught up in their thoughts that they mistake them for their identity. This is a huge mistake. The type of thought you think can be triggered by various causes: your upbringing and family beliefs; the media; society; the mental state you are in; medication; food; drugs; sleep issues; mental health issues; physical health issues; hormonal imbalances; chemical imbalances; your surroundings; and habits- to name a few.

Stop believing everything you think!

Your mind is similar to a radio. It can play different stations based on the frequency you tune it to. When you are in a negative mood, you are in a lower frequency (or state of waking trance) and you are more likely to think additional negative thoughts and feel further feelings of negativity.

When you are in a positive frame of mind, this frequency can produce happier thoughts, as well as positive energy. It gets the creative juices flowing and you experience more pleasurable feelings. This is because everything is energy, including your thoughts, feelings, words, and outcomes.

The more you fill your mind with inspiration and positive influences, the fewer depressing thoughts you will have.

Truth be told, everybody has negative thoughts flowing through their minds throughout the day. The main difference is that some people have come to realize that they can choose to replace unwanted thoughts with something entirely different.

The more you think negatively, the more you are programming yourself to continue thinking this way. Do you notice how it can feel corny and futile to think positively sometimes? According to Dr. Joe Dispenza, your body can actually become addicted to the emotions produced by your thoughts! Breaking a negative thought cycle and creating positive transformations will feel slightly awkward in the beginning, because you are forming new habits and wiring new pathways in the brain.

How Can You Turn Your Thoughts Off?

The more you try to stop your mind from thinking, the more frustration you will experience due to your mind resisting and seemingly becoming busier.

The key is to learn how to turn the volume down- not turn it off. You will be able to transform your thought process overtime, with daily practice, using methods provided in this book.

To have a healthy mind, you also have to take care of the body. And vice versa. Both are connected and have an effect on each other.

Please note: If you are dealing with negative thoughts, especially thoughts of self-harm or harming others, you need to seek medical attention immediately.

What is the Placebo Effect?

It is likely that when you hear the term, "placebo effect," you mistake it to mean deception or trickery. The placebo effect is medically documented proof of just how effective the subconscious mind can be at creating profound results when it is led in a specific direction.

There are many scientific studies that demonstrate the power of our inner mind. For instance, studies have shown that around 34% of people with hypertension in a clinical trial responded positively to being administered sugar pills, showing a documented decline in their blood pressure measurements.[1]

Clinical trials using placebo pills prove how your beliefs can activate your internal chemical reactions, producing a measurable change in cases involving symptoms of pain, fatigue, depression, anxiety, IBS and some symptoms of Parkinson's.[2]

Your expectations contain a significant amount of power to create noticeable results in all areas of your life. In fact, according to Ted Kaptchuk, a professor of medicine at Harvard Medical School, and one of the leading researchers on the placebo effect, there is documented evidence that you can still obtain remarkable results even when you know you are taking a sugar pill!

One of Kaptchuk's studies in 2009 reported surprising numbers of participants doubling their rates of improvement with symptoms of IBS, even though they knew they were taking fake pills.[3]

Unfortunately, the opposite of the placebo is also true and just as potent. This is known as the nocebo effect- when your brain anticipates negative side effects from a pill and you end up experiencing those unwanted symptoms. Even sugar pills can cause non-desirable side effects if that is the outcome you anticipate.

The action of taking a pill, even a placebo, causes your brain to anticipate outcomes and create results based upon your expectations.

The placebo effect is the power of your mind.

Use this knowledge to your advantage. Boost your results by unleashing the placebo effect in your life without using placebo pills by training your mind to anticipate the outcomes that you *want*. Shape your expectations in a positive way.

Do that by using a mantra, such as:

"Something wonderful is about to happen."

"Results are on their way. This is going to work."

Why Should You Connect to Your Subconscious Mind?

You must change what is in your head before you can change what is in your hand. Your beliefs alter your results.

Have you seen how even the most disobedient of animals will completely transform when they spend time with someone who understands them (such as a dog whisperer, or a horse whisperer)? The same thing can happen for your mind- it can function in harmony when its basic needs are met.

Whether you experience times when your mind seems to get stuck in a negative rut, or you feel like you are not using your mind to its maximum potential, you can start to become your mind's very own whisperer, honing in on its basic needs, commands and desires. When you do this, you will start to feel more harmony, inner peace, enlightenment, self-certainty and empowerment. You will start to see the infinite possibilities of your potential unfolding around you.

Flip the Switch

When you are in Survival Mode, you seek pleasure in the moment, which does not necessarily bring you the things you want, especially long-term happiness. When you make the switch to Thrive Mode, you know that facing challenges, pushing yourself and taking care of yourself will lead to the things you want, including lasting happiness, which can also provide pleasure in the moment.

In Survival Mode, you struggle to take care of yourself and have low energy and negative patterns, which will lead to a lot of unwanted results. In Thrive Mode, you can take care of yourself, and others, while having bountiful energy and positive patterns, which lead you to fantastic results.

Once the switch happens, you will feel it, as if there is a source of energy springing forth from within you. This is the ultimate state of being in alignment with your mind, the universal energy and the things you want. There are several methods to do that without having to consume a huge chunk of your time or energy. This book will teach you methods to do that.

Chapter 3
Command Your Power

I was sitting in a conference, in a room full of highly achieved business owners and entrepreneurs. A friend of mine owned a thriving business and he had invited me as his guest. I was seated near the back of the room, watching the crowd as they jumped up and cheered each other on, handing out high-fives like Kool-Aid.

Then I felt a tap on my shoulder. I turned around to see a large man, at least twice my size, peering down at me. I gulped.

"Come with me," he said in a stern voice. My first thought was, 'Did I do something wrong? Am I in trouble?' However, I took a deep breath, got up from my chair and followed the big man to the back of the room, wiping those concerns from my mind.

"I have heard of the work you do, and I am wondering," he paused, staring down his nose at me, "are you able to speak in front of my business team and help them? I would really love if you could do that."

I tilted my head back to meet his gaze. 'He has heard of my work!' I felt thrilled- this guy was a big deal. "Sure, we can discuss the details. What time-frame do you have in mind and approximately how many people?" I asked.

"Now and in front of anyone who is here," he gestured out to the crowd.

Yikes. I had two options: one, kindly say "no," as I was just a guest at the conference and had absolutely nothing prepared; or, two, say "yes" and see where this adventure took me. I took a deep breath, connected to my inner power, feeling nudged towards what I must do.

I looked the man boldly in his eyes and said, "Yes. This is going to be great." With no plans, not even a clue, I stepped in front of the crowd and delivered a presentation, pouring my heart into it. At the end, they were all begging for more!

I was so grateful I knew how to flip a mental switch, connect to my power and feel as though I was being guided to where I should be and what I should say. Can you imagine what it would feel like to be able to do this type of thing for yourself, upon command?

How to Connect to Your Subconscious Mind

Just like any muscle in the human body, the more you use your subconscious mind and your intuition, the stronger they will get and the easier they will become to access.

Pretend you are to set a goal of being able to do 100 push-ups without stopping. If you have not done push ups before (or even if it has been a long time since you have done one), you will need to break the goal down into a plan of action consisting of smaller bite-size chunks, such as starting with 10 push-ups the first day, increasing the number by a specified amount each following day, until you reach your goal.

The first few push-ups you do over the first days or weeks will feel slightly awkward and this may cause you to doubt your abilities, your form or the goal you have set. By sticking to the plan, with time and practice, the push-ups become easier and before you know it, you have reached your goal and now you have certainty in yourself, your abilities and your potential.

Of course, you could adjust each day's increment depending upon how fast you want to reach your goal of 100 push-ups, or how you are feeling. The main thing is that when you have a plan in place, and you have accountability, you are more likely to push yourself and go further.

If you are a go-getter and would like additional support and accountability to reprogram your mind to get what you want, I can help you with that. I have online programs and communities to help you accelerate the process at www.feelingpowerful.com/go. You will also find links to join me on social media.

What is Trance?

Trance is a naturally occurring altered state of the mind where distractions seem to fade into the background, while your mind becomes focused. There are different levels of trance, which the mind fluctuates through, throughout the day.

You are in some form of a trance every day, sometimes at a lighter level, sometimes entering deeper. For example, have you ever been so caught up in a daydream that you lost track of time and forgot about your surroundings? Have you ever experienced driving somewhere, only to realize upon arriving at your destination, that you were not consciously paying attention the whole time? Have you ever been "in the zone" where everything seems to run so smoothly, and you feel as though you are performing at your best?

Those are all examples of being in a state of waking trance. You can also enter a waking trance through silence and meditation, music, performing habits and routines and via exercise and movement

A deeper state of trance feels so wonderful that people crave it, especially once they learn how to enter this state for themselves. In a deeper state of relaxation, your mind will feel calm, focused, recharged, clear and fluid. This is the ultimate state of communicating with your subconscious mind, where you will hear your intuition and you will experience your creative juices surging. This is the state of enlightenment and self-discovery- empowering you to become who you are. If you want to master your mind, yourself or your life, you must learn how to enter a productive state of trance yourself.

The more you practice connecting with your subconscious, the deeper you can dive into trance and the better you will feel, during and afterwards.

What to Do When Your Mind Starts to Drift

At first, as you start to work on controlling your mind and entering a deeper state of relaxation, you may notice resistance and distractions. Rest assured, this is normal. Your mind will start to drift because this is what it got away with for all these years, and it is now a natural tendency. You can change this.

Each time your mind drifts away, catch yourself in the action, and bring your awareness back to your breathing. It helps if you imagine breathing light and love into your body. When you exhale, do so through your mouth and picture yourself releasing tension, stress and worries- as if you can push it away with your breath.

How Will You Know You Have Connected?
When you connect, things start to click.

*Please Note: Many methods within this book require you to:

1. Be safely seated with your eyes closed. Do not use any of the methods within this book while driving or operating machinery.
2. Be in a quiet place where you will be undisturbed.
3. Practice them several times until they become automatic.

Method # 1: Warm Up

Create focus, calmness, balance and become present to the moment.

Instructions*

1. When you are safely seated with your eyes closed, inhale deeply, filling up your lungs.
2. Exhale through your mouth, pretending you are fogging up a mirror in front of you, exhaling fully.
3. Repeat two more times. As you inhale, imagine calmness and light entering your body, following your breath into your lungs. As you exhale, visualize stress and tensions leaving your body. Open your eyes after the third deep breath.

Use this technique throughout the day to help yourself create balance and bring your awareness into the present moment. I will walk you through this process at www.feelingpowerful.com/resources.

In the initial phase of connecting with your inner self, you will notice your breathing slowing down, your heartbeat slowing down, your focus increasing, and calmness spreading throughout your body and mind. Your body may start to feel heavier, as if your muscles are melting into your seat- or, for some people, they begin to feel lighter, as if they are pleasantly floating. You may also notice the temperature of your body shifting to slightly warmer or cooler. And, just as in REM sleep, your eyelids may move rapidly while in this state.

The other sure sign of being in an enhanced state of trance is that discomforts within your body will melt away. Deeper states have a natural anesthetic affect.

Within a few minutes of being in this state, you can feel as if you are a battery that has been recharged. You may even start to notice a greater sense of connection within yourself and the universe.

Eventually, you will go into a deeper mental state, where you will have command over your subconscious mind. Your senses can become heightened in this phase. You will begin to have ideas and solutions come to your mind. This can happen via images, words, thoughts or feelings. It occurs differently for everyone. Once you are connected to your inner self, you will be more in tune and able to discover how your mind speaks to you. Pay attention to it; it is always communicating with you. However, it is likely being drowned out by loud music or background noise or thoughts or self-doubt and fear.

Enter Powerful Mode and Unlock Your Potential

Your mind is your superpower.

I used to be one of the most skeptical people. At one point, a friend of mine made me watch a popular movie about the Law of Attraction and my response at the end was, "Thanks for wasting my time with that load of garbage."

The ability to renew our minds and recreate our lives? Nah, that's up to fate!

Or so I thought... until I found myself on the path of self-discovery. I desperately desired to fix the broken parts of myself- the negative thinking, bad habits, self-sabotage and depression. Which led me to finding hypnotherapy.

As much as I loved learning hypnotherapy, I didn't believe it. One time our instructor, in a demonstration, made all the students believe their eyes were glued shut. As intriguing as it was, I didn't experience anything. My eyes opened to the sight of one of my peers frantically waving his hands out in front of him- his eyes firmly closed. His eyebrows were twitching up and down, as he struggled to open his eyes, but was unable to do so.

All I did with my eyes at that moment was to give them an exaggerated roll. I was the one in the classroom who said things like, "Yeah, right, he's probably faking it."

So, I naturally did what anyone would do... I tested my new skills on friends and family (once I was certified, of course). Unbelievable things started to happen.

"I have the funniest story to tell you," Stewart boasted, full of excitement and unable to keep a grin off his face. "I can't even believe it!" He was one of the first people I ever hypnotized.

Stewart was built big and sturdy, towering above me. "I'd love to hear it," I eagerly replied.

"You know how you programmed my mind to feel extremely happy every time I form a fist with my right hand?"

"Of course," I said.

"Well the other night I was at work and my co-worker started making me very angry. He was really getting on my nerves with the way he was speaking and behaving, as if he was trying to push my buttons. I had reached my limit. I was going to punch him in the face.

"But when I made a fist, I suddenly burst into laughter and felt so good. All the anger and annoyance disappeared. It confused the other guy so much that he backed off and left me alone! I guess I'll be keeping out of trouble from now on!" We both laughed at the irony in Stewart's resolution of the situation. The hypnotherapy really worked.

Basically, Stewart now had a physical trigger that was programmed to produce a phenomenal feeling. I call this the "Happiness Button," and I will teach you how to program yourself with this button later in this book.

Wouldn't that be incredible, to be able to program your mind to flip your mood, just like that?

Chapter 4
The Ultimate Mind Hack

I will start by saying this: there are no shortcuts to the results you want. Put in the work, or it catches up with you in some way and it will hold you back from your goals. Yet, for my clients and myself, the following strategy has *felt* like a shortcut.

The best strategy to produce a state of trance and "hack" into your subconscious mind quickly and easily is hypnotherapy- the therapeutic use of hypnosis.

You have seen how hypnotists can produce profound results by hypnotizing a volunteer to believe in something so much that they experience it as if it is real- because it *is real* to their subconscious minds.

Allow me to teach you some insider secrets that make hypnosis so effective. Throughout this book I will reveal secrets of a hypnotist, which you can apply to yourself, experiencing real changes within your mind. Do you see what an advantage this will be for you- to be able to program your mind so proficiently that you believe in a new reality- instantly? Can you think of the endless opportunities you will have with this knowledge- being able to hypnotize yourself to be more confident, better at closing sales, increase your courage, feel happier, and create new healthy habits for your own success? Those are just a few ways. You will discover more as you continue reading this book.

Revealing the Top Secrets of a Hypnotist

"Why is it that I self-sabotage?" Earl asked me, staring me straight in the eye. He was a savvy multi-millionaire who owned several businesses. His suit likely cost more than the average person's paycheck. Although Earl was in the top 1% of the world's wealthiest people, his income had reached a plateau and he had remain stuck there for a few years in a row. "My income and my weight have plateaued for the last few years despite my best efforts. The harder I try, the more I feel stuck."

He then listed the areas in which he was sabotaging himself. Have you also experienced times where it felt like part of your mind was holding you back?

Of course, there are many reasons a person will sabotage their own success. From what Earl had already told me, it was clear to me that he was very self-aware and humble enough to admit when there was an issue. I could see that Earl was in a coachable state, open to suggestion and he was eagerly awaiting my advice.

I leaned forward, meeting his gaze, and said, "Let me teach you a few of the core secrets of hypnosis. Once you know them, you will gain more control of your mind."

A few months later, he proudly marched up to me, grinning from ear to ear. "No more plateau! My body is the fittest it's been in years and my income has more than doubled- and it's still growing!"

Would you like to know what I taught him? Throughout this book I will be sharing my techniques and I will be letting you in on the secrets that make hypnosis so effective.

Hypnotists' Secret # 1:
The Power of the Subconscious Mind

Hypnotists do not possess any more power than the average person. They simply utilize their knowledge of the subconscious mind effectively.

This is good news for you. This means you can learn to be nearly as effective at programming your subconscious mind as hypnotists are. Keep in mind, Hypnotists go to school to learn these skills and they practice them continuously.

Have You Been Hypnotized Before?

When you think about stage hypnosis, you probably remember stories about people doing something embarrassing, and then telling everyone after the show that they remember nothing about what happened.

And now you are wondering, "Does hypnosis really work?" Well, let me ask you this… When I mention stage hypnosis, what is one of the first images that pops into your head?

Your answer is probably either somebody clucking like a chicken or a man dangling a pocket watch and intoning, "You're getting very sleepy." I am not reading your mind. I am merely showing you that these responses demonstrate that your mind has been conditioned (hypnotized) to a certain extent, already. Hypnosis is everywhere- via suggestions and conditioning- so, the more you learn about your mind, the better off you will be.

Below are a few examples of common beliefs that are firmly planted into people's subconscious minds from a young age, and continue to influence their everyday lives.

"I'm not good enough."

"You have to finish everything on your dinner plate before you can leave the table. There are starving children in Africa."

"The early bird gets the worm."

"Money doesn't grow on trees."

"It's my way or the highway."

Do you see how those beliefs can shape different areas of your life?

If you are not the one in control behind the steering wheel, who is? And more importantly, where are you going?

Is Hypnosis Dangerous or Evil?

There is a common misconception that hypnosis is from the devil or that you have evil powers if you use it.

Do you remember when people used to say yoga is dangerous and evil because it opens your mind to spirits? How about when people used to think medicine and operations were evil? All of these have become common and acceptable around the world, as society is advancing.

The mind often fears what it does not know, and what it perceives to be different.

What is Hypnosis?

Hypnosis creates an altered state of mind, commonly known as trance, in which the conscious mind is bypassed, and the subconscious mind becomes highly receptive to suggestion.

While people have reportedly been entering states of trance since the time of the ancient Egyptians, hypnosis became commonly used by physicians in the 18th century, using it as a form of anesthetic during surgeries and even amputations. It was practiced in modern medicine up until anesthesia was discovered.

After that, it was kept alive by stage hypnotists (for entertainment purposes, only) and is now finding its way back into modern hospitals throughout Europe, because of its therapeutic benefits. In fact, some of those hospitals have incorporated the use of hypnosis in place of traditional anaesthetics. This is called "hypnosurgery."

During hypnosis, distractions fade into the background and the mind becomes extremely focused, while the body feels pleasantly relaxed and free of discomforts.

When you have several programs running on your computer, what happens? It causes your computer to malfunction. When you shut down all the programs except for one- your computer's function often improves.

The same can be said for your mind. Being in a deep state of hypnosis feels as if you can shut down all the programs running in your mind and focus on one thing at a time.

Some people can achieve a similar mental state in meditation.

What is the Difference Between Hypnotherapy and Guided Meditation?

Think of it this way, hypnosis is like meditation, but, on steroids.

Both hypnotherapy and guided meditations have similarities: they are guided, and they use visualizations to relax the body and calm the mind, and access a deeper state of relaxation (trance) in order to increase the feeling of overall well-being.

However, the main difference is that with guided meditation, you may enter trance at some point and the instructor may not know exactly when or how you will do that, while with hypnosis, the hypnotist knows when and how you will enter trance.

Meditation, especially for beginners, is sort of like getting into a car and driving around, with only a vague idea of what route you will take to get there. Hypnosis is like getting into that same car, but having an exact destination and using a short-cut to get there.

Hypnosis uses targeted words and techniques to access your subconscious mind, and reach your goal. During hypnotherapy, the internal beliefs can be accessed, replaced and updated.

Can you see an obvious and tremendous benefit to using hypnotherapy?

Either way, both meditation and hypnosis (when used correctly) are great tools to learn how to control your mind.

If you are anything like me, you do not like wasting time, you like to get right to the point and you want to be more productive… which is why I prefer hypnosis and refer to it as the magic bullet for programming your mind to get what you want.

Do you find that your mind is busy, and you have difficulty slowing it down enough to meditate? Hypnosis is a much easier method for you to gain control of your mind.

Hypnotherapy is a frame of mind that can be used to retrain the mind.

Can Anyone Be Hypnotized?

Yes. However, everyone will experience it differently.

Maybe you have noticed this- during a stage hypnosis show, the hypnotist will ask for volunteers and bring a group of people up onto the stage. He will then execute a few quick hypnosis-inducing methods, going to each volunteer, one at a time, and giving their hand a quick pull with the command: "Sleep!"

Many of the volunteers will close their eyes and appear to fall asleep, even having their body become so limp that they are keeled over in their chair. Yet, you will notice that there are always a few people who sit there with their eyes open, looking bamboozled after the stage hypnotist tells them to sleep.

You might be thinking that the hypnosis did not work or that those people are un-hypnotizable. This is what most people think, but, that is incorrect.

There are several reasons why they did not go into a trance. Perhaps their mind required a bit more time to enter that relaxed state, or they were not following the hypnotist's instructions fully because they were nervous about what might happen, or they were slightly uncomfortable with being on stage and afraid they might do something embarrassing against their will. The more analytically-minded people tend to require a few more conditions to be met before they can enter a deep state of hypnosis.

The people who are most suggestible and therefore react the best in stage hypnosis shows are the ones who are more easily able to use their imagination. Everybody's mind functions in different ways, so, everybody will experience the effects of hypnosis in different ways.

Let me ask you this: what is it you expect to feel, in order to know for certain that you were, indeed, hypnotized?

Most likely, your answer is this: you expect to go into such a deep state that you lose all consciousness of everything that is happening, including yourself and what the hypnotist is saying to you. When you come out of trance, you expect that it will be as if you were under anaesthesia- where you have no recollection of what happened, whatsoever.

At the very least, you expect to feel like you have no control and that you must follow everything the hypnotist says to you and that you end up clucking like a chicken, unable to stop yourself.

Be honest, is that what you think it feels like to be hypnotized?

If that is the case, you have been misled. However, the fact that you assume those things about hypnosis proves that *you have been hypnotized* to give that response. Your beliefs and expectations were shaped, somewhere along the way, and now you have a certain opinion about something you have never even experienced for yourself.

Even if I tried to explain hypnosis to you, it won't do it justice. That would be like describing what chocolate tastes like to somebody who has never tried chocolate before.

Hypnotists' Secret # 2:
The Power of Knowing Your Audience

In this case, your audience is yourself. To get the best results, it is helpful to know how your mind interprets instructions and how well you follow through with them.

Hypnotists must know how suggestible people are, in order to hypnotize them, which means hypnotists tend to have an acute ability to read a person's body language and their suggestibility. When you can read how a person is feeling, you can almost predict what they are thinking, as the mind tends to stick to patterns. When you understand the patterns, you are better able to bring a person into the conversation and get them engaged in what is being said.

How Suggestible are You?

How you will experience hypnosis depends on the way you interpret the world around you. The general categories of suggestibility are listed below. You did not get to consciously choose which category you ended up in. This was developed before you were seven years old, depending on how your parent figures treated you and how you interpreted it.

The main types of suggestible people are:

Physically Suggestible

This type of person takes everything literally. They act now, think later. They use their body to protect their emotions. Physically suggestible and extroverted, they like to be the centre of attention. This type of person is more sensitive to physical touch, and has an easier time imagining physical sensations, such as what it feels like to accidently touch a hot element on the stove. They have an easier time following instructions, meaning they can more readily enter into a deeper state of trance and experience what most people would expect to experience from being hypnotized.

Physically suggestible people are therefore more likely to act out what they are imagining, making them very entertaining to watch in a stage hypnosis show.

Emotionally Suggestible

This type of person takes everything indirectly, reading between the lines. They want to think about things for a while, then act later. They tend to be analytical, rational and logical. They use their emotions to protect their body. They are introverts, preferring to blend in with the crowd.

Emotionally suggestible people like to have control and are more likely to question instructions or outright reject the instructions, because they do not like being told what to do and prefer to do things their way. These people can still be hypnotized deeply, however, they tend to care more about what other people think, plus, their mind is always analyzing everything, and their guard is always up, so, they will not act out what they are experiencing within hypnosis.

The process of hypnotizing this person requires more time and a different setting than stage hypnosis. Because they do not experience hypnosis in the way that they expect to, they often do not think the hypnosis is working, until they practice it a few times and become more familiar with the process.

The Split

Nobody is 100% one or the other type. While having characteristics of both suggestible types, people will tend to lean more towards emotional suggestible or physical suggestible. Some people fall into the category of a 50/50 spilt between being emotionally suggestible and physically suggestible. People who are in this category are, obviously, a mix of both the two suggestibility's, which can sometimes make them difficult for other people to read.

The Exceptions

Yes, there are exceptions to every rule, including your level of suggestibility. The main exceptions are: how much affection you received from your parent figures as a child; your surroundings when the suggestion is given; who is giving the suggestion and the amount of perceived authority they have over you; your willingness to follow the suggestions: and the current state of mind you are in.

Would you like to know the state of mind that causes you to be the most open to suggestions?

Fear. When you are scared, your logical mind is bypassed and sensations become heightened. When someone told you a scary story, did you feel chills up and down your spine and the hairs on your arm rise up?

When you are fearful, your mind is open to suggestion, and your rationale will likely go out the window. Can you think of a time when you were scared and you made a bad decision or you were not able to act the way you normally do? Fear took over and changed the way you think and behave. At times when you feel like you have no control in your life, do you notice how you are in a state of fear?

Fear is powerful enough to stop you in your tracks and make you do something abnormal. Think of the areas of your life that are being controlled by fear. Do you have a fear of missing out? Fear of rejection or failure? Fear of success? Fear of scarcity- that there is not enough of something for everybody? Fear of heights, snakes, or small spaces? Fear of being alone with yourself and finding out who you really are and what you can achieve?

If you want to learn to master your mind and take control, you will have to learn to pay attention to the things that scare you, because those are the things that control you.

Which do you fear more: failing and feeling embarrassed and hurt because of failing or being rejected; or the fear of living an unlived life, full of regrets and sadness?

If fear is in the driver's seat, it is time to take the wheel like your subconscious mind depends on it... because it does. Your subconscious mind needs you to take control, for you to get the most out of your life.

Who is Easier to Hypnotize: a Person with a Closed Mind or a Person with an Open Mind?

People with closed minds form opinions about things they know nothing about. Because of their closed minds, they tend to be stubborn and stuck in their ways. Generally, they do not follow instructions well, which means they do not follow the hypnotist's suggestions, resulting in a resistance to being hypnotized. It is not that they cannot be hypnotized- it is that they choose not to be.

Open-minded people, on the other hand, want to get more information before they form an opinion. They are open to guidance and willingly follow instructions, trusting their gut instincts as to which leaders to follow and which ones to ignore.

Are YOU Hypnotizable?

Here are a few questions you can ask yourself, in order to get an indication about whether you will feel the effects of hypnosis in the same manner as the volunteers in a stage hypnosis show.

Do you get goosebumps when somebody tells you a heartwarming story?

Do you often get lost in a daydream and you lose all sense of time and your surroundings?

Are you able to focus so intensely on something that you lose track of time?

When a friend tells you a story and describes the details, are you able to imagine it taking place in your mind?

Do you ever find yourself making hand gestures while you are having a conversation in your head?

Have you ever caught yourself talking to yourself out loud?

If you said yes to any of those questions, it is an indication that you are capable of entering a deeper state of trance, as you are effortlessly able to access your imagination and empathize with others.

Some people are not readily able to tap into their imagination, so, it may take several sessions of practicing and training the subconscious to willingly enter a deeper state of trance. This is usually true for people who are always very analytical and feel the need to remain in control.

However, just as you can train your body to run a marathon, you can train your mind to become more accessible and responsive- especially to your own suggestions (except it will be much easier than training for a marathon!).

Practice the methods provided in this book, even if you do not feel what you expect to feel during hypnosis. You will still get results. With time and practice, you can train your mind to go into a deep state of hypnosis.

What Does Hypnosis Feel Like?

You know what it feels like just before you fall asleep at night, where images are flashing through your mind and your body feels like it is melting into your bed like warm butter on a hot piece of toast?

When hypnosis is used therapeutically, it can feel extremely relaxing for both your mind and body, as if you closed all the tabs in your mind and gave it a peaceful break. But, describing hypnosis to someone who has never formally been hypnotized before is like describing to a deaf person what the waves of the ocean sound like. That is not so easy to do, right?

If you are curious about what it feels like to by hypnotized, allow me to help you. I will provide you with my most popular hypnosis audio program for *free*. Just go to www.feelingpowerful.com/resources and sign up to gain instant access.

How Effective is Hypnosis?

As mentioned previously, everyone will experience hypnosis in a different way. A small percentage of people who are very suggestible will experience everything and a small percentage of people who are very analytical will not experience much. Most people lie somewhere in between- they will experience many of the suggestions, but possibly not every single one of them.

The efficacy of a suggestion depends on several factors, including your surroundings, your upbringing, the way you perceive the world, the way you understand and follow suggestions, how easily you can tap into your imagination and relax (vs how much you resist), what medications you are on, and if you are experiencing mental illness, among others.

What is Hypnotherapy?

While hypnosis uses suggestions in an altered state, hypnotherapy is the combination of hypnosis and therapy in order to locate the inner beliefs that are holding a person back and reprogram their minds to achieve success at reaching their goals.

Hypnotherapy is often used to access repressed memories and emotions, to change the way the mind processes information, such as past traumas or issues that are happening in the present.

What is Hypnotherapy Commonly Used for?

- Overcoming fears and phobias
- Increasing self-confidence, self-worth, and self-esteem
- Stopping habits and behaviours, like smoking, nail biting, overeating, and cravings
- Optimizing sports performance
- Developing skills to cope with stress, anxiety, nervousness
- Instilling calmness and relaxation
- Boosting motivation
- Improving sleep quality
- Pain management
- and more

Hypnotherapy is a method of training the mind to create both a new thought process and new behavioural patterns.

When I help my clients to achieve their goals, I am usually *de-hypnotizing* them. This means I am helping them to remove the outdated and faulty inner beliefs that are holding them back from what they want.

You will learn more about this in the second pillar.

How Effective is Hypnotherapy?

Hypnotherapy has been shown to be very effective; however, its level of success depends upon a few factors, such as: the level of the hypnotherapist's training and skill, how suggestible you are, and how well you follow instructions. Keep in mind, if there was a one-size fit solution for everyone, the world would have no issues.

Using hypnotherapy, I have been able to successfully:

- Change cravings and food preferences entirely (from craving sugar and chocolate, to craving vegetables and meat)
- Overcome Binge-eating disorder
- Alter my thought process from negative and powerless, to optimistic and powerful
- Redesign the way I feel daily
- Change my habits, actions and behaviours
- Alter my preference for exercise (from hating exercise, to loving it and genuinely looking forward to it)
- Change my unconscious reactions, such as habits and dealing with stress
- Find an instant way to boost my confidence, mood, productivity, creativity and happiness
- Get into the zone, on command
- Create a life of purpose, meaning and fulfillment

Plus, I have helped my clients to do the same for themselves, transforming their entire frame of mind, feelings, actions, behaviours and of course, surroundings (meaning results!).

Should Everyone Be Hypnotized?

While hypnosis and hypnotherapy can be beneficial, it is crucial to do your research before seeing a hypnotist or hypnotherapist. These are unregulated industries in many places in North America.

There is one possible negative side effect to hypnotherapy. As hypnotherapy is often used to uncover repressed memories, there is a chance a poorly trained hypnotherapist could suggest a false memory, which you believe to be real. Adequately trained hypnotherapists will know not to do this.

Always be sure to get diagnosed by a medical physician before starting any new treatment. If you have epilepsy, or extreme mental disorders, such as hallucinations, suicidal thoughts or personality disorders, hypnotherapy may not be for you.

To get the results you desire, it is important that you trust this person before proceeding. Hypnosis is a very effective tool, so if you are going to use it, I recommend to only be hypnotized by a credible person and to avoid the rest.

Why would you willingly open your mind to somebody you *do not* trust? Stop doing that!

If I'm Being Honest...

Think about the last time you watched a movie or episode of a series. Did you watch it because you were truly interested in it, or because someone recommended it to you and you saw a lot of people talking about it online?

Hypnosis is all around you. Or more clearly stated, suggestions are everywhere. Everything around you is a form of suggestion and some of them are more hypnotic than others: music, social media, advertisements and commercials, to name a few. Your friends suggest to you which apps to download, which restaurants to eat at and what movies to see. The news suggests the world is mostly made up of crime and daily natural disasters. The media suggests that you are not cool enough or happy enough- but that you can increase your popularity and your confidence with a nicer car, bigger house, more followers and a flashier lifestyle.

Making Suggestions that Work

Suggestions become highly effective when they are repeated frequently or given by an authority figure to another person who is in an altered state. Authority figures include (but are not limited to) doctors, police officers, politicians, celebrities, experts, parents and teachers. If you look up to someone and view them as being superior to you, they have a certain degree of authority over you.

You enter a more suggestible state of trance when your guard is down while your mind is focused on something else, such as when you are daydreaming, in the zone, have your eyes fixated on an object, focused on empathising with someone's story, or feeling overly emotional- to name a few examples.

Combine that with an authority figure who is giving you suggestions and your mind is likely to become a fertile garden, allowing seeds of suggestion to be planted and take root. Can you see how your mind naturally goes into altered states of suggestions throughout the day, whether you think about it or not?

When you are watching T.V. (it is called T.V. programming for a reason), you are in a suggestible state of waking trance, soaking up what you are watching and programming your mind. And you often believe what we see on T.V., right?

Another common time you are in a suggestible waking trance is when you are scrolling through your social media newsfeed. You usually do it on autopilot. Would it be fair to say you frequently find yourself checking your notifications and scrolling unconsciously through your newsfeed?

Take a moment to think about the people you fill your feed with. If you compare yourself to an account and it brings you down, unfollow that account. If the account inspires you or motivates you, follow more accounts like that. The people you follow have a direct effect on your mind and mood. The more attention you give them, the more influence (and power) you are giving them. Decide who is worth giving that much of your power to.

Think about what your account is doing for your followers. You can be the trigger that creates uplifting feelings within other people.

Can You Hypnotize Yourself?

Yes, and this is exactly what I will teach you how to do, via self-hypnosis. Many people fear they will get stuck in hypnosis and be unable to respond if the fire alarm comes on or the phone rings. This is false. You will remain aware while hypnotizing yourself. However, you may fall asleep if you are tired or too comfortable. Rest assured (pun intended), you will wake up refreshed and be out of trance.

Can you do hypnotherapy on yourself? Hypnotherapy is difficult to practice on yourself because your conscious mind will most likely be in the way of the unconscious programs (your deepest internal programming). You can, however, use the self-hypnosis method below to use the power of hypnosis to make huge changes for yourself. To get the full results of hypnotherapy, it is best to work with a professional hypnotherapist. Keep in mind, I was trained to do hypnotherapy, so, my skills will be more expansive and more effective compared to yours.

I will provide you with a method to effectually hypnotize yourself, access your subconscious mind and plant positive seeds of suggestion into your own subconscious mind.

Before I teach you my self-hypnosis method (the same one I teach my clients), I want to show you several ways in which you are currently already hypnotizing yourself (and probably experiencing unwanted results, because of it!). I will also let you in on some secrets of the hypnosis industry which will help you to productively program your subconscious mind to get what you want.

Self-hypnosis is a self-controlled state of mind.

Chapter 5
Hypnotize Yourself

There is so much wisdom right in front of your face that it is often overlooked. When you were younger, you learned to spell. Ironically, the words you speak are akin to spells. Your self-talk is a form of suggestion, which means you are engaged in self-hypnosis. Yes, you can hypnotize yourself. This is something I teach to all my clients, empowering them with this remarkable edge for life.

How often do you say things like, "I'm so bad with names," "I'm trying my hardest to quit that bad habit," or "I'm broke"?

Hypnotists' Secret # 3:
The Power of Words

Hypnotists know that the conscious mind and the subconscious mind both tend to understand the same sentence in different ways and there are certain words that trigger immediate reactions within the subconscious mind.

Example 1: Although it may appear that the volunteers are sleeping while they are in a deep hypnotic state, they are not actually asleep- they are merely experiencing a peaceful and restful state of trance that has similarities to REM sleep (when the mind is dreaming).

The hypnotist will use the word, "Sleep," when giving suggestions because the subconscious mind understands that word to mean, "relax, let go, rest, close your eyes, be still, allow your conscious mind to drift away." You can see that it is much

> shorter and easier to say the word, "Sleep."
> Example 2: In stage hypnosis, the hypnotist tells the stage volunteer, "You are glued to your chair and no matter how hard you try, you remain stuck to that chair. In fact, the harder you try to get up, the stronger the glue becomes." The person's upper body moves and their legs kick a bit as they attempt to stand, but they remain cemented to the chair. A look of surprise comes over their face. They wiggle some more but still cannot budge. Then they give up and look at the hypnotist in confusion. What did the hypnotist do in order to produce such incredible results? There are certain words that the subconscious mind will understand differently than the conscious mind. Think of it this way: there is part of you that needs logic and another part of you that likes to dream. Both of those parts of the mind will understand the same sentence in a different way.
> The hypnotist told the person, "You're glued to the chair and remain stuck...." That is the first suggestion. Then the hypnotist said, "The harder you try, the stronger the glue becomes." There is a hidden suggestion within that sentence, and it is not entirely about the glue becoming stronger.

How to Get Results like a Stage Hypnotist and Change Your Life

Would you appreciate it if you could get results like a stage hypnotist for yourself? Keep in mind, Hypnotists take courses on this and put in a lot of practice. However, you can experience dramatic results for yourself by applying the techniques I am about to teach you.

Think of the limitless doors that you can open with your mind, being able to hypnotize yourself to be confident, release stress and tensions, increase relaxation, change your attitude, boost personal productivity, feel happier and so much more... It is almost as if you have entered a secret chamber with countless doors before you. It is up to you which door you choose to open next.

Using Effective Suggestions to Hypnotize Yourself

What happens when I say: "Do not think of a purple monkey sitting in a tree." What image just popped into your head? A purple monkey sitting in a tree. That is because that sentence contained a negatively embedded suggestion.

The following table lists some common negatively embedded suggestions that you may be communicating to yourself. From a hypnotist's standpoint, I have provided better suggestions to swap with any of the negative suggestions you may be currently using.

It is said that, "I am," are the two most powerful words in the English language because what you say after them shapes your destiny. This is because any time you use the words, "I am," you are essentially using self-hypnosis; you are making suggestions to your subconscious mind.

Negative Suggestion (replace these phrases)	Effective Suggestion (the replacement phrases)	Reason
"I'm losing weight"	"I am letting go of the excess pounds" "I am releasing excess weight"	What happens when you lose money or your cell phone? Your mind panics and does everything to find it because it feels horrible. With weight, how often do you lose the weight, and gain it all back… and then some?
"I lost ten pounds"	"I released ten pounds" "I am ten pounds lighter"	Same as above
"I am starving"	"I'm so hungry, I want to eat now"	Your mind has been conditioned from

		the periods of starvation your ancestors lived through. These words put your mind into a frantic state, causing it to want to stock up and eat more.
"I have so many flaws"	"I have some areas that are stronger than others"	The Law of Awareness: Only suggest to your mind what you want and focus on that.
"Don't forget to call me"	"Remember to call me"	The Law of Awareness: suggesting forget or remember to your subconscious
"This is going to be so difficult"	"This is going to be a good strength-building challenge"	The Law of Awareness: suggesting difficulty or strength
"Never give up"	"Stay strong. Keep going"	The Law of Awareness: suggesting giving up or pursuing
"Never miss a meeting"	"Show up to every meeting"	The Law of Awareness: suggesting missing meetings vs attending them. Are you seeing the pattern?
"I have so many problems"	"I'm facing a few obstacles"	"Have" implies ownership. When you own something

		your subconscious wants to keep it!
"I'm stressed"	"I need to take a break and relax"	Science shows how even just saying the words, "I'm stressed" can increase the amount of stress you are feeling.
"I quit smoking"	"I have stopped smoking"	From a young age we are taught that quitting is bad, so the subconscious does not like to be a quitter
"Bad things always happen to me"	"Good things are on their way"	The Law of Awareness: Suggest what you want
"I hope I don't mess up in this presentation"	"I will do well in this presentation"	Same as above
"I hope this contract doesn't fall through"	"I hope this contract succeeds"	Same as above
"I don't want to stay awake all night"	"I want to get a restful night's sleep"	Same as above
"I'm so bad with names."	"I am working on improving my memory. Can you remind me of your name, again?"	I am calling you out. Forgetting names is usually BS. You forget the names because you did not care enough to pay attention when the name was being said and not putting enough conscious

		effort into remembering because you were too busy being in your own head and thinking about yourself.
"She is a pain in my neck"	"She is challenging me to grow"	Be mindful of suggesting illness, pain, harm and negativity upon yourself
"He makes me sick to my stomach"	"He's not my favorite person to be around"	Same as above
"I died when I saw this"	"I was completely shocked when I saw this"	Same as above
"This is killing me"	"I'm not a fan of this"	Same as above

Hypnotists' Secret # 4: The Power of the word "Try"

This is perhaps the most important secret of a hypnotist that I am revealing to you. Going back to the previous example of the volunteer being stuck in the chair, while the conscious mind may hear, "Try to get up," the subconscious hears, "Fail at getting up (stay stuck)." Hypnotists know that to the subconscious mind, the word "try" means the same thing as "fail."

Do you want to know what's funny about this scenario? All the hypnotist has to say for the volunteer to become unstuck and get out of the chair is, "Alright, you may stand up now," and the person will be able to stand up with ease. The hypnotist understands the impact of using the right words.

If words are that powerful, what unwanted results do you think you create in your life based on what you tell yourself? When you

> say something like, "I'm going to try," you are actually telling your subconscious mind, "I have decided to fail."
> Think about it, when someone asks you if you can make it to their event and you really do not want to go, what is your response? "I'll try to make it." You know full well this means you are not going, am I correct?
> Stop using the word "Try." If you are halfway committed to your goals, the subconscious takes that to mean that your goals are unimportant to you and that you want to continue failing at them.
> There are other words and phrases that have an alternate meaning to the subconscious mind, as well. The most commonly misused words and phrases are listed in the following chapter.
> Instead of hating the game, become better at playing it.

Returning to Earl's story of experiencing self-sabotage, the more he noticed he did it, the more he repeated the story of himself holding him back from his bigger goals. He continually told this story to himself and the people around him, most likely, reinforcing it. Of course, the first step towards changing an unwanted behaviour is to acknowledge it.

Yes, you should admit when you have a problem and talk to people about finding a solution to it. But then, you must become able to catch yourself when your mind is focused on the story, repeating it, expanding upon it and feeling the emotion tied into it. The stories you repeat are a form of self-hypnosis-you hypnotize yourself with the things you frequently tell yourself.

Cut those ties! Become aware of the things that are holding you back, catch yourself before you run the entire story in your mind, and create a new story, instead. You are not changing the events, details or facts about the story. You are changing the way you tell the story. We will get more into this topic later in this book.

Are you beginning to see how you may have been unconsciously self-sabotaging?

Mindset is everything. Change your mind, change your life.

Observe the patterns in your mind. Become aware of them and come up with more effective suggestions, which align with your goals and ambitions. Start by using a couple of new phrases at a time in order to prevent overwhelming yourself. Forget about perfection and focus on progress.

Be mindful of what you tell yourself because over time your mind will start to believe it.

I sat down with Devontée, a Canadian artist who composes his own music in the hip hop/rap genre and he told me how much he believes in the power of the mind. You can imagine me sitting across from a hip hop/rap artist- there is a night and day difference between our looks.

Yet, we had one major commonality: our careers are both centered around our voices and words (me, through coaching and hypnotherapy; Devontée, through music).

This artist wisely told me, "Words have power. I never write into my music anything that I don't want to have happen for myself."

Whether it is a question of the law of attraction or a law of the subconscious mind, words have potency. Be mindful of what you say to yourself and others.

"Power is control and patience. To be in control of your thoughts and body; whatever you want to do, you can do it. And patience is big because you can have all the power, but if you have no patience you can lose it all." Devontée.

Become Your Own Super Hero with Self-Hypnosis

While using this method, you will always remain in control. However, you may become so relaxed that you fall asleep. That is nothing to worry about- this occurs during meditation for some people, as well. Rest assured, you will wake up and feel refreshed afterwards.

There is a time and a place to go into a deeper trance, depending upon what you are looking for. However, work on remaining awake during self-hypnosis, so that you can experience more of what your mind has to offer.

Are you ready for a way to make your affirmations sink into your unconscious mind? I will teach you how to do that, using my super, simple self-hypnosis method. This will be like affirmations on steroids (metaphorically speaking, of course!).

Hypnotists' Secret # 5: The Power of Vocal Emphasis, Tone and Pace
Hypnotists know when to speak loud or quiet, fast or slow, and to act out the scenario with their voices. Think of somebody who is an entertaining story-teller. Their voice speeds up and gets louder when they are talking about something exhilarating, they slow down and they speak quietly when they are saying something sad, and they demonstrate the emotions through body language. The audience gets the full experience of the story, feeling it as if they were there, themselves.

Method # 2: Self-Hypnosis

Connect with your subconscious mind, enter trance and plant positive suggestions.

To make self-hypnosis the most effective for you, I recommend using the same music that I give to my clients. It contains binaural beats and helps to focus the mind. You can have instant access to a 90 minute track I created at www.feelingpowerful.com/resources.

(Refer to the diagrams below).

Instructions*

1. Sit in a safe and comfortable position in a quiet place and close your eyes.

2. Focus on your breathing. As you breathe in, imagine calmness entering your body. As you exhale, pretend you can release your cares and worries, out of your mind and out of your body. The more you focus on your breathing, the more relaxed you feel.

3. Imagine you are at the beach- it is right in front of you. However, before you can reach the sandy shores, you will need to descend the staircase before you. In a moment you will slowly walk down those stairs, but before you do, take a moment to

properly assess them. There are ten stairs in total. They are well lit, comfortable for your body and you feel safe.

With every step down the stairs, pretend you can go deeper into relaxation and deeper into your subconscious mind. With every step down, you feel more focused, calm and peaceful.

Slowly count from 10 down to 1, saying the words, "deeper relaxed" after every number, like this, "ten... deeper relaxed... nine... deeper relaxed... eight... deeper relaxed..." Continue until you reach the bottom.

4. After stair number one, imagine seeing a treasure chest right by your feet. Visualize yourself opening the chest and say, "I choose to access my inner power now."

Visualize the scene in your mind becoming brighter, like a light turned on. Pretend you can feel power lovingly radiating out of the open treasure chest and into every inch of your body.

It is almost as if you have become a super hero by opening this chest.

5. Insert your intentions and suggestions for what you want. Use an affirmation of your choosing and repeat it ten times. Here are a few examples you can use or alter to make your own:

- "I am now connected to my subconscious mind and infinite possibilities await me. I can do anything."
- "I have what it takes to reach my goals. The path is now unfolding before me."
- "I am confident, powerful, beautiful and intelligent."
- "I am good enough. I am worthy enough. I am enough."
- "I am better today than I was yesterday."
- "I am in tune with my subconscious and following my intuition."
- "I choose to make today the best that it can be."

6. *Feel* your affirmations. Use emphasis and emotion- even if you are doing this all in your head. Emotion must be used in order to make this effective.

7. Once you feel a shift in your emotions, return to the stairway and start to slowly ascend the stairs, counting from one up to ten, saying the words, "Wide awake," after each number ("One… wide awake… two… wide awake… Three… wide awake…") Do this until you reach number ten.

8. Open your eyes and notice how rested and powerful you feel.

You will see that I instruct you to use the words, "Wide awake." Keep in mind, while in a state of trance, you are not asleep. However, your subconscious mind understands the words, "Wide awake," to mean, "feel alert, energized, aware, focused, present, etc." Remember, we are working with the rules of the subconscious mind, here.

This process will take some practice. Of course, it works better when there is a hypnotherapist to guide you through it. I teach all of my clients self-hypnosis and it is a tool they use for the rest of their lives. If you would like me to help you with the process, my guidance is available in an online program. It will help you to make sure you are doing this method effectively so that you can achieve optimal results. Accelerate your journey and master self-hypnosis at www.feelingpowerful.com.

Power Now

Diagram 3: Entering Self-Hypnosis

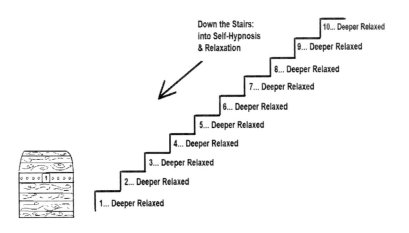

Diagram 4: Accessing Your Subconscious Mind

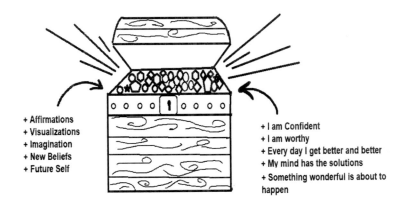

Diagram 5: Exiting Self-Hypnosis

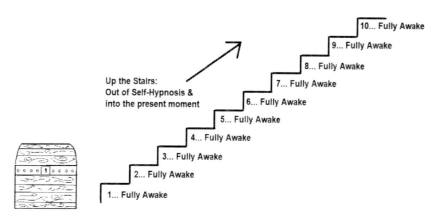

Once you have connected with your mind, your mind will start to respond and become your servant, instead of you serving it. This experience can start to feel like you have found a genie in a bottle. Instead of three wishes, you are granted the ability to command your mind and program your mind to help you reach your desires.

This is not an overnight solution to all of your needs. You must put in practice, patience, persistence and perseverance. Some people will notice results faster than others and this is due to several factors, such as: some people can go into self-hypnosis deeper and easier; some are more ready to see results; some self-sabotage; some practice this method daily; and some people are very inconsistent and impatient.

I recommend using this self-hypnosis method at the beginning of your day to set your intentions for the day, create focus, balance and a possibility mindset.

Now that you have practiced hypnotizing yourself, you are ready to start with training your subconscious mind to give you answers and solutions.

Chapter 6
Connect to What You Want

Method # 3: Spark Creativity

Use your subconscious mind to form ideas and find solutions. The solution is within.

Instructions*

1. Connect with your mind using the self-hypnosis method from Chapter 5. Once you get to the bottom of the stairs and open the treasure chest (step number four), proceed as follows.

2. Give your subconscious a specific command.

Example: "What is the solution to ___ problem? (Fill in the blank.) Please show it to me and help me solve it."

3. Wait in silence for a few moments, removing expectations.

You know how when you forget the name of something and you are put on the spot and you cannot think of what it is called, but you know that the answer will come to you later in the day when you are not even thinking about it? The answers will come when you remove the pressure and trust that your mind is processing your request in its own time.

4. Be patient.

I use this genie in a bottle method all the time. If I misplace my phone, I connect with my mind and ask it to remind me of the last place I was holding my phone. An image will appear in my mind, I will go to that location and sure enough, there is my phone.

Truthfully, the answer may not pop into my mind right away. Depending upon the size of my request and goal, it can take minutes, hours or days. However, the answer always does appear in my mind eventually and it is always an innovative solution when it shows up.

Are you beginning to see how useful these methods will be in your everyday life? Continue to use all these methods to gain the ability to access your subconscious mind easier, faster and on deeper levels. This is just the very beginning of an exciting adventure that is sure to come.

Focus Pocus

If you stop and think about it, although there are many distractions, the problem is not that people need more focus. They are already focussed on checking their social media notifications, worrying about what other people think, fearing the worst case scenario and mentally replaying problems on repeat. This is less of a problem to do with lack of focus and more of a problem to do with focussing on the negative.

Hypnotists' Secret # 6:
The Power of Focus

Whatever you choose to focus on, your mind will expand upon and you will experience more of that.

People who have entered a deep trance will often tell you how impressed they are with the level of focus they had- not even the audience's laughter distracted them while they were in trance.

Imagine being able to focus so intensely that you are undisturbed by sounds as loud as crowds laughing at you! How would your life look if you were able to do this on command? When you train your mind to attain a deep level of focus, such as trance, you will be able to tune out the distractions and tune in to your goals.

Method # 4: Clarify Your Goals

Know what you want and connect to it.

Instructions

1. Get a pen and piece of paper and think of the dreams that you would like to fulfill. Write your goals in the present

tense, as if they have already come true, placing the words, "Thank you," at the beginning of every sentence.

2. State what achieving that dream means to you, what it allows you to do, or how you feel having reached it.

Example: "Thank you that I attract the best people into my life, allowing me to have the most satisfying friendships and the happiest memories with my loved ones."

"Thank you that my business earns $X (list your goal amount), which allows me to travel, feel inspired, and expand my business to help more entrepreneurs."

"Thank you for my strong, healthy, fit and happy body that allows me to move about freely and comfortably, enjoying every aspect of life."

3. Continue to list all your goals.

4. Repeat this daily, giving it time to sink into your subconscious mind and sending your mind in the direction of your dreams.

Make sure you always have a goal in sight. Your goal = your vision.

You can always change your goals.

When you connect to your goals (or a specific goal) you are setting an intention and giving your mind direction. When you connect to a goal that is bigger than yourself, (uplifting and inspiring you), you are programming your mind to live a life full of purpose, fulfillment and happiness.

Life's Most Important Questions

Many people focus on "Why am I here?" or "What's my purpose?" and those questions cause you to feel stressed and stuck, instead of enlightened.

Method # 5: Gaining Clarity on Your Purpose

Do you ever feel like you do not know your purpose? That is O.K. Many people feel that way. It is not necessary to know your purpose in order to live a purposeful life. If you really want to get the most out of your life these are the important questions to continuously reflect upon.

1. When do I feel happiest?
2. What do I want from my time here?

3. What is most important to me?
4. If today were my final day on Earth, how would I want to spend it?

If your answers are motivated by wanting to please others or live up to what they want for you, cut through all the BS. This is about YOU. Your well-being, happiness and fulfillment are your primary job. Yes, job- not hobby.

There are many people who will go their entire lives without ever knowing who they truly are or what they can achieve. Meanwhile, you are here, reading this book, seeking your best self and diving deeper into the realms of possibilities. That is something to feel proud of.

Method # 6: The Power of Surrendering

Connect to your subconscious mind, always do your best, and learn to surrender the rest. You will begin to experience your power to the fullest, when you know how and when to surrender.

Instructions*

1. Connect to something bigger than yourself.

You can rely on a higher power, your faith, your goals, your passions, your purpose and your plan of action. If you do not have a plan to get to where you want to be, or you want to accelerate the process, hire a coach. These days you can receive guidance with just about any goal, so there is no excuse to do things alone.

2. Let go of what you cannot control.

In all honesty, even when you are the best version of yourself, there will still be times where things happen that are beyond your control. You will encounter tough times or challenging situations- that is part of life.

Use an affirmation, such as repeating to yourself, "Let it go," and use techniques to help your mind move forward, while releasing the negative. There are techniques provided later in this book.

3. Change your mindset.

When I become stressed, I shift my mindset by asking myself two questions:

"Does it change the situation or become any better by me feeling stressed out right now?"

"If today were my last day on earth, would I want to waste the last few moments feeling upset?"

Truthfully, stress only wastes your time and emotions, robbing you of precious time where you could be happy or creatively seeking a solution.

Do feel overwhelmed, lost or stuck? Do you feel that having a bit of guidance could push you past the obstacles and help you to step it up and become the best version of yourself? Are you wondering, "Where do I begin and how do I get started?"

If you are anything like me, you do better when there is professional guidance and structure. Make things as simple as possible for yourself by committing to your goals and focussing on one thing at a time.

Start your day by developing the habit of creating a winning mindset for yourself. This will initiate the snowball effect throughout your day. When you begin your day by winning your morning and winning your mindset, you are setting yourself up to be victorious at the end of the day, too.

How many times has the day started off poorly or you have woken up on the wrong side of the bed and wished there was something you could do to fix it?

You know how good you feel when you start the day strong, right? Your entire day seems to run smoothly. So, why not do that on purpose? You can use hypnosis to program your mind to be focussed, productive, positive and successful. Mornings are usually a tough time for a lot of people… But, that can change! And it can happen in a matter of minutes per day.

Remember, hypnosis is a way of recharging your mind and helping you to feel rested, focussed and energized. Doesn't it make sense to start your day that way? Let's do that together. Join the movement at www.feelingpowerful.com.

PILLAR 2
CLEAR

Chapter 7
What the FORK?

"Why the fork am I still single? I don't forking understand!"
A woman (let's call her Susie), cried to me- except she was not using the word "fork." Susie was cussing like a sailor. Anger, frustration and desperation were beaming out of her, as if she were radioactive. "I have forking tried everything and I am a good person but there are no forking, decent, single men lining up to date me. Why the fork, not?" she yelled at me. I felt the need to back up a bit, as if her words were knives being thrown at me.

This was the first time I had met her. It was off to a bad start, wouldn't you agree? It was almost as if she needed someone to be angry at and blame for her being single. She was pretty, petite and in healthy shape. Her outfit was professional and stylish. Her outward appearance was most definitely not the cause of men avoiding her like the plague.

Susie had been rambling on for a few minutes now, spewing out cuss words and hatred like a monkey throwing its own shit around. Who would want to be around someone who is this negative? She continued, "I paid an energy worker $3,000 to clear away any energetic reasons as to why the fork I am having no forking luck with finding a forking man to marry me!"

"STOP where you are!" I interrupted. Her mouth froze mid-sentence and she stared blankly at back at me. She was in her fifties- how could she fall for something like that? Desperation. It changes people and can cause them to do stupid things. Here Susie was, sitting in my office, looking me in the eye, practically screaming, and flooding the room with her putrid attitude.

I continued firmly, "Stop talking. It's my turn to talk, now." I was grateful this was a consultation, because this is *not* the type of person I accept as a client.

Anger and desperation are understandable. However, acting like a victim, pointing blame at others for your problems and hurling your negativity at the world are unacceptable. I could see that, although Susie was in a state of trance, repeating her story and living it as if it were happening in the present, she was not in a coachable state. She was looking for someone to blame and someone to take responsibility and give her an overnight fix. Sadly, this means that she is likely to inflict more pain upon herself because she is unwilling to see her part in this and do what it takes to make a change.

However, that did not stop me from being hopeful and planting a suggestion that would someday come to fruition for her. "I will give you one extremely valuable piece of advice, and I will give it to you for free, not $3,000…" I said.

I was preparing her for the blunt truth. Sometimes we need a reality check to get out of the patterns within our minds that are holding us captive without us being aware of it. I took it one step further, saying calmly, "You can't pay someone to take away your problems. If you want real and lasting results, you must do the work, yourself. The best thing you can do is to work on what is happening internally for you; the anger and resentment must be dealt with if you want to attract men.

"Even if you do not act this way in front of them, these thoughts and feelings are probably flowing through you most of the time, which men will feel, even on a subconscious level. Whether they are aware of the reason or not, they will feel repelled away from you. If you want to attract quality men and become alluring, you must clear that baggage away, first.

"When you become luminous, happy and loving on the inside, it will pour out of you and others will feel it. You obviously believe in energy; it's time you take responsibility for the energy you are putting out into the world. Invest in learning techniques to clear away the self-hindering patterns and replacing them with a positive and attractive internal belief system."

Susie's jaw had dropped open and she sat there frozen and in silence for a few minutes… before she said, "Fork this! I don't need to change! I paid the energy healer to do all of that for me. All those men need to change- they're the problem." With that, she stormed out of my office.

I guess I did not give her the answer she was looking for, refusing her the justifications she tells herself as to why she does not need to change. If I am being honest here, it is fair to say nobody would want to be around somebody like that- especially not the decent, dream man that she is seeking. He is definitely out there, and he exists… but I can guarantee you he is fleeing away from that type of energy.

Susie simply cannot hurl her heavy baggage at other people and then blame them when they do not want to carry it for her. These days people are becoming more self-aware and enlightened, realizing that useless baggage can be thrown away and replaced with something lighter and more pleasant.

This baggage I am referring to is the negative mental and emotional programming that is inhibiting Susie from reaching her goals. Susie is not alone- we have all picked up some unnecessary luggage along the way. Sure, it will take some time, effort and learning some new-found skills to find the burdening baggage and throw it away.

However, what do you think will be a more difficult and unpleasant in life for Susie: remaining stuck in her old ways and repelling her goals away; or going through the process of creating change and programming herself to attract her goals towards her?

You do not need a $3,000 energy healer to tell you that your thoughts and emotions have a direct effect on the way you feel and the way others feel around you. Invest that money elsewhere by realizing this: you can attract what you want.

But, first you must clear the junk out of the way and make room for what you want.

Chapter 8
Clear Limiting Past Programming

The Benefits of Pillar 2: Clear
- Silence the inner critic and replace it with self-belief
- Remove internal limitations, get unstuck and get flowing
- Overcome unwanted patterns, such as self-sabotage
- Replace unwanted habits with healthy ones
- Release uncomfortable emotions and express yourself
- Remove invisible barriers and attain inner peace and enlightenment
- Increase your ability to control your mind
- Gain skills to cope with stress and deal with negativity
- Remove negative energy and influences, opening room for positivity

Clear the Way

In pillar two, you will learn effective methods to clear the negative mental programming of the:

1. Past: Limiting Programming
2. Present: Negative Conditioning

It makes it difficult to get from point A to point B when there are beliefs and behaviours that are creating resistance and holding you back. This would be like trying to drive to your destination without realizing the E-brake is stuck in the on position. The entire car is not broken- it simply requires mechanical attention.

Before I teach you my best strategies to clear the way, there are a few things you should know.

Why You Need to Clear Your Subconscious and Make Room

Pretend you have an old couch that is stained and falling apart, and just looking at it makes you cringe. You consider buying a new one. Say that you find a modern couch that is the style you want, it's comfortable and you know that it will instantly brighten up the whole room. So, you buy it and you feel good about the recent purchase.

When you get home with it, and bring it inside, you notice there is no room for it because the old couch is still there. You could attempt to move the furniture around the room... But, you know it is going to be too crammed and uncomfortable, which, kind of defeats the purpose of the new couch in the first place, right?

You have three options:

1. Try to return the new couch, and keep the old one. But, let's be honest, you will never be able to get rid of the image of the updated couch, or how it made you feel, so, you end up trying to distract your mind and numb your emotions. And you complain about how things never work out for you.

2. Keep both pieces of furniture, creating an uncomfortable space that does not work, and the whole flow of good energy is now off balance and just being in that room pisses you off. And you complain about the new couch not working for you.

3. Get rid of the old sofa, creating room for the new one and bask in how bright, modern and uplifted your place has become. You replaced the old with the new and this change feels so good, the only thing to complain about is wishing that you made this change a long time ago!

The couch in this example represents your internal beliefs- your programming. All couches will get worn out and outdated at some point, needing to be replaced. Your beliefs can serve you for a long time... until they are no longer serving you and they need to be replaced or updated.

When you are honest with yourself, you will know when you have reached that point.

It is important to know that the beliefs and habits that you have are not your fault. The beliefs were handed down to you, as I mentioned at the beginning of the book. You had no control over how you were raised and the events that happened to you throughout your life. However, the great news is that you can overcome unwanted habits and outdated beliefs. You can take charge and give yourself the opportunity to become the best version of yourself. That version of you already exists, here, in the present. You must uncover that self by removing the baggage that is in the way.

Unconsciously, you have committed to particular mental patterns because they helped you to cope in the past, as a means of helping yourself. They worked for a time and got you to where you are, however, you experience times of being stuck or feeling that invisible barrier holding you back because you continue to apply the same old formula, hoping that it will bring you new results.

If you want a different outcome, you must change the formula and now is the time to do that.

New formula = new results.

Your beliefs influence who you are and how you live your life. They are sneaky and can pop into your mind, tricking you into thinking that voice is your own, causing you to believe it. Even though society and technology have advanced so much, the subconscious mind still has many primitive beliefs. You will be able to see which ones run throughout your family. It is up to you to stop the hindering beliefs from being handed down into the future generations.

Keep in mind, while there are some beliefs that hold you back, you have many beliefs that attribute to your great qualities and characteristics. This chapter is mainly addressing the beliefs that hold you back. Here are a few examples of natural tendencies of the mind that have been transmitted unconsciously through generations.

Watch Out for these Thought Patterns

Start to become aware of the common thoughts that are running through your mind. Are you noticing a common thread? Do some of those thoughts need to be dealt with?

Below is a list of a few typical thought patterns that tend to run through the mind:

Not Enough: "I'm not _____ enough." Insert what comes up for you: worthy, good, skinny, rich, young, old, talented, etc.

Lack Mentality: "There is not enough ____ for everyone."

Happiness is Somewhere Else: "I will be happy when I get _____."

Resistance to Change: "I will start the process tomorrow."

Perfectionism: This appears in the form of waiting for the right timing, or for the perfect job, spouse, or conditions so you can feel happy, take time for yourself, or take the next step towards your dreams. "I cannot ____ until I _____." Example, "I cannot hire a coach until I am more successful."

Need for Familiarity: "Why do things need to change? I was just getting used to things the way they are." Resistance also shows up in the form of, "I'm going to keep doing things my way (thinking the results will change without the actions changing)."

Need to be Right via Justification and Excuses: "I can't because _____." Justifying where you are and why you are not where you want to be. This can go a long ways, such as finding the one article online that has something bad to say about your new game plan, causing you to ignore all of the hundreds of good articles and reviews. "I just knew it would be bad- look at this article!"

Worry: "This worries me so much." Worry is misusing your imagination to expand upon problems or create issues that do not exist.

Need for Blame: "I wish the universe would just give me a sign, already." This is a form of passing off responsibility, because if things go sour, then there is someone or something to blame.

Need for Validation and Approval: "Oh, it is 11:11 right now. This is a sign from the universe that I am on the right track."

Patterns and Meaning: "It's 11:11! Everything happens for a reason." Does everything happen for a reason, or do you attach a meaning to it? Your mind will have the tendency to attach a meaning to everything. You can use this to your benefit: always attach a meaning that will uplift you, empower you and transform you.

"I'm stuck. I'm not good enough. Nobody cares about me. Things never go my way." Those beliefs got you to where you are- do you see that they cannot get you to where you want to be? Do you agree that it is time for those negative paradigms to be replaced with positive ones? Are you ready to alter your internal mental formula?

Method # 7: Let it Go

Imagine the biggest obstacle that is in your way. Is it low confidence, a bad habit or a limiting story you keep telling yourself? Get out a piece of scrap paper and write that problem down. Make sure you do this!

Once you have done so, crumple that piece of paper and squeeze it into a ball, squeezing it as tight as you can. As you continue to clutch even tighter, imagine your hand is becoming glued shut. Your hand is closing so tightly and is becoming rock solid. Tighter and tighter.

As you keep clasping your hand shut, notice how your hand is beginning to feel. Maybe you are beginning to feel tired from the tension? Does it hurt you to keep holding on?

Now, you can let go and release your fist. Let your fingers loosen. Do you feel how your hand naturally wants to stay in a crumpled position? Does your hand feel tired and weak, making it slightly difficult to fully open?

Let me ask you this: What hurts you more- to continue holding on to that issue, or to let it go?

In which areas of your life are you holding onto problems and excuses and inflicting pain on yourself? Are you looking for any excuse as to why you cannot succeed? Are you seeking any reason as to why you should not change?

Most importantly, are you ready to give yourself permission to release the problem? Are you ready to overcome the fear? Will you allow yourself to break through and finally have what you want?

Throw that ball of paper across the room, saying goodbye to that challenge. Give your hand a good stretch. Do you notice how your hand feels lighter? Do you see that it has recovered and is free to do so much more, now that it is open? Will you commit to your success, even when the pain of change appears, knowing that you will feel all that much better and lighter after getting through it?

Stop waiting for somebody else to give you permission to change, move forward and succeed. Give yourself permission to let go, stretch, gain your strength and open to the potential and freedom that is awaiting you.

Now is your time.

Method # 8: Reframe Your Past

You cannot change the past... However, you can reframe it. Reframing is a common technique used in hypnotherapy in order to help you recognize a past memory with a different understanding of it, thereby revising the way you feel about it. This can be done on a conscious level, too.

In the past there was a time when somebody you were close to hurt you and let you down. Your mind will naturally cling to that pain, shock and betrayal, replaying that memory and seeing yourself as the victim. If you allow yourself to stay in a state of victimization you will prevent yourself from healing.

The other person hurt you and may have done something wrong- that is a fact. This cannot be changed. However, the part of your mind that dwells upon this past hurt is your ego, which is gnawing on the negative emotions you are experiencing. The only thing you can adjust about this event is the way you see it. By doing so, you can create a positive ripple effect in your life, starting with the way you feel.

You must realize, we are all humans and all of us make mistakes. We are all products of our programming. As audacious as this may sound, when someone hurts you, put yourself in their shoes and think about where they were coming from and what lead them towards their actions. This does not make them right for doing so; this helps you to forgive and heal. Can you see that this person may have acted out of their own pain, fear or insecurities? They have their own troubles, which caused them to act the way they did. Yes, they should have dealt with it in a better way. However, they dealt with it in the way they knew how. Perhaps their parents treated them that way, too.

This does not justify their actions. What they did was hurtful, yet you cannot reverse it, so it is up to you whether you want to hold onto the unsettling feelings or do yourself a favor and let it all go. Healing takes time and effort.

Instructions*

1. Use the self-hypnosis method. Once you get to step 4 of the method, proceed to the instructions below.

2. Think of one challenge that you are currently facing, or one memory that is triggering uncomfortable thoughts and feelings within you. Example: a time when somebody hurt you, a time when you failed or got rejected, a time when things did not go as planned and you lost hope, etc.

3. Ask yourself: "What is the blessing or the lesson that I got from this situation?" Make sure you find the answer before moving on to the next step.

4. Apply forgiveness. Forgive all who were involved in that memory, including yourself. Forgiveness is an act of releasing yourself from invisible chains that are imprisoning you. It is not for the other person, it is for you. Say, "I forgive you. I forgive myself. Thank you for the lesson." This can either be said aloud or within your mind.

5. Advise yourself. Imagine that the current version of yourself can go back in time to the past version of yourself in that specific memory. If you were able to give yourself some advice, what would you say to yourself to help you release those

negative feelings? What can you share that will make your younger self feel happy and safe?

You must make your younger self feel better in that past memory before you can move on.

6. Change yourself. Tell yourself, "Life is not happening *to* me, it is happening *for* me," and ask yourself, "How will I become a winner because of this moment?" Find your answer.

7. Change your feelings about that memory. Focus on how you will come out ahead because of this challenge. Visualize yourself being filled with love and light, and imagine they have the ability to pull the negativity out of your body, cleansing your body and mind and leaving them both feeling refreshed and renewed.

8. Visualize the future version of yourself being unaffected by this challenge. Imagine yourself being in a better position because of this lesson. Say to yourself, "Thank you. I love you." Spend a few moments here basking in the wonderful feelings.

9. Bring those wonderful feelings into the present moment and count yourself out of self-hypnosis, using the self-hypnosis method.

This is a process that you will have to repeat in order to create a breakthrough and get past negative mental programming. This technique is more effective when you have an expert guide you through it.

While working on de-hypnotizing yourself of the limiting beliefs from the past, become aware of the factors that are hypnotizing you in the present.

How will You Know if You Still Have Limiting Beliefs?

Diagram 6: The Garden of Your Mind

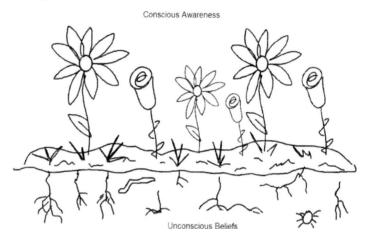

There is no such thing as a garden that never grows weeds. You cannot tell what is beneath the soil just by looking at the surface. In time, you will see what is growing and you can continue to pull the weeds from the root, and plant more seeds of what you desire. Be on the lookout for internal programming that is still holding you back. Just because you went through this process once, does not mean all of the negative and outdated beliefs will be removed from your mind. There will likely be several hidden beliefs in there.

However, a vigilant gardener can be on top of the weeds and notice them when they first sprout above the ground. The weed can be pulled right away before it takes over the garden.

Truth be told, your mind will continue to experience negative or uncomfortable thoughts and emotions from time to time. The goal is to turn that voice's volume and frequency *down* and to acquire skills to cope with the challenges and come out on top, like the champion that you are. With vigilance, that voice will have less power and you will have more.

Here is a not-so-obvious and major indication that you still have limiting beliefs:

Do the following visualization. Mentally fast-forward into the future and picture yourself having already achieved your goal. If you still feel unfulfilled, then you have more work to do. Visualization is your imagination, so, if things are not sitting well in your imagination, that indicates that there are parts of your mind still dealing with internal conflict.

How will You Know When You Have Successfully Reprogrammed Your Mind?

When the new programming has taken place within your subconscious, there will be a few indicators. Plus, you will notice a ripple effect within other areas of your life.

The obvious signs are that the unwanted behaviours are no longer there (or they are diminished), and that you are experiencing desirable results (or have reached your goals). The process of moving towards your goals can start to feel easier, faster and more enlightening.

Some patterns can change overnight, and some will take more time to overcome. Remember to be patient with yourself.

Chapter 9
Clear Current Negative Conditioning

Does Brainwashing Still Exist?

In the 1890's, the Nobel Prize winner and Russian physiologist, Ivan Pavlov conducted an experiment with dogs and food. He noticed that the dogs would start to salivate when they perceived certain triggers that they had come to associate with food, such as the lab assistant entering the room. When he rang a bell the dogs did not respond at first. Then he started ringing the bell whenever he fed the dogs until one day the dogs started to salivate whenever he rang the bell, even though there was no food. The dogs had learned to associate the bell with food and their involuntary response had become conditioned within them.

In a similar way, you have been conditioned, too. This is part of your programming. And the conditioning occurs daily through your thoughts, words, self-talk, actions, habits, internal programming and surroundings.

Hypnotists' Secret # 7
The Power of Repetition
You will often notice hypnotists repeating key phrases. The mind likes repetition and the more something is repeated, the more familiar it becomes. The mind sticks to what is familiar. You condition yourself through repetition. Are you willing to begin conditioning yourself to become who you want to be and live the life you have been dreaming of?

Can an Old Dog Unlearn Old Tricks?

Does conditioning last forever? Interestingly, Pavlov discovered that his dogs' conditioned response could become unlearned, as long as conditions changed. Pavlov would ring the bell without giving the dogs food to see what happened. Over time, the dogs stopped salivating when they noticed no food appeared after the sound of the bell.

Humans live most of their lives in a state of autopilot- doing everything out of habit. Which means that by changing your habits and directing them towards your goals, you can reprogram yourself over time to get more of what you desire, because habits can be both learned and unlearned. The subconscious mind likes habits because it likes to follow patterns and stick to what is familiar. Use this to your advantage and invest a little time each day towards developing a habit that will bring you closer to what you want.

When it comes to deprogramming your mind of old beliefs and reprogramming yourself for better outcomes, give yourself plenty of time and repetition. The choices you repeatedly make, the thoughts you frequently dwell upon, the actions you persistently take and the stories you commonly tell yourself are all ways in which you are conditioning yourself. Those are all forms of self-hypnosis.

Condition your mind to be happy, confident and successful. You can overcome just about anything. It is your mind that you have to convince and you can do that through positive repeated self-conditioning.

Your World is Filtered

Have you ever forgotten where you placed your sunglasses and started frantically looking everywhere for them, only to feel stupid a few moments later as you realize they are in your hand? How is it that you were unable to see them or feel them, even though you were focussed on finding them? It comes down to the filtration system in your mind.

Your mind is constantly filtering out the stimuli from the external world around you, as well as your thoughts, emotions, past experiences, memories and knowledge. You are not continuously consciously aware of the feeling of your clothes against your skin, your stomach digesting your lunch, the first time you fell off your bike and every last detail in your surroundings. While all of these things are real, they are being filtered on an unconscious level, based upon what is most important for your survival. You were so focussed on your sunglasses being elsewhere, that you were unaware of the fact that you were already holding them.

This means the mind can glaze over the truth, seeing only what it is programmed to see. Your expectations can shape your experience. Just because you are unable to see it, does not mean it does not exist. It only means it is non-existent in your awareness.

What do Facebook and Your Mind have in Common?

Facebook is known for its "unique" filtering system. Say you are looking at your newsfeed and you see an update that someone you knew a few years back just had their first baby. You press the 'like' button out of courtesy. Facebook sees that you liked this update, which has a picture of a baby, assuming you must really like babies and the next thing you know, everyone on Facebook is having babies!

Anytime you interact with somebody else's status, Facebook takes it to mean you want to see more of that topic or person, so it filters out a majority of everything else. Go through your friend list and find someone who you have not seen an update from in a long time. While it is possible they have not posted in ages, it is more likely that Facebook has sifted them out of your newsfeed.

This comes into play when people are outspoken about topics like politics and global events, which can make it seem as if everyone in the world shares the same views and opinions. In reality, Facebook has given you biased opinions based upon what you are interacting with.

Whether you agree with those or not, this social media site sees that they get a reaction out of you, and Facebook's whole goal is to get more of your attention; therefore, you will see more of those types of posts.

Before you know it, you are only seeing updates from a small handful of the same people, instead of the entire list of friends you wanted to keep in touch with. That bias will affect the way you think, feel and behave.

Your mind filters things in the same way. Your beliefs shape your perspective. Your past programming affects the way in which you view the world and yourself. You do not see the world as it is, you see the world as you have been programmed to see it. You do not even see yourself entirely as you are because of your past programming. You live as the person you *think* you are, while possibly never knowing who you *really* are. You must discover and remove outdated beliefs to uncover your authentic self.

What does Your Life have to do with the Car you Drive?

A good example of this filter is what I like to call the Blue Car Effect. Recall the time when you purchased your vehicle. You proudly drove it off the lot and excitedly started cruising towards your home. Along the way you noticed there were a few other people also driving the same vehicle and, as it happens, also the same color. Over the next week, you are still thrilled about your new ride, but you are noticing something strange. You are seeing so many of the exact same vehicle everywhere you go. Did a whole bunch of people purchase the same vehicle that week?

No. Your new ride is merely at the forefront of your mind, creating a sort of filter, making this exact vehicle more noticeable to you. In fact, there are no more of your vehicle on the road that week than there were the previous week. Your mind now has a bias based on your awareness. Your awareness can be used as a tool. Whatever you are aware of, you will experience more of. What you focus on will become more in focus.

The good news is that you can always shift your awareness to that which you want, which will direct your mind and subconsciously suggest that you experience more of it. When you train yourself to switch your awareness, you are picking up the beneficial skills for accessing your inner potential.

This is not the fake motivational stuff telling you, "Just think positive!"

You need to change more than your thinking to create the life you want. You must take inspired action on a consistent basis. The motivation for that comes down to the way you think: your mind will either be motivated to avoid pain (ex: loss, failure, humiliation and rejection); or to seek pleasure (ex: wealth and thrills). More often than not, the mind is motivated by avoiding pain.

Use the power of your conscious thoughts and awareness effectively by either thinking of a solution for your unwanted situation or adjusting the way you see the situation. When you alter your perspective, you unleash the possibility for dynamic transformations in your life, because this will influence a shift in your motivation and behaviour, allowing you to revise your actions and your outcomes.

Focus = Power... are you beginning to *see* that?

Whatever you choose to focus on, your mind will expand it and create more of it- this a law of the subconscious mind. Your conscious awareness engenders a subliminal suggestion for what to feel and experience in any given situation.

Your choices and your decisions are your ultimate power. You always have the choice to innovate the way you think and feel during any circumstance.

Reshaping Your Mind and Redesigning Your Life

I was fifteen and volunteering at a community event in a room packed full of a few hundred people. My job was to hand out free T-shirts. Sounds like fun, right? I was impressed that people would get a free shirt, just for walking by. As I was handing out the shirts, saying, "Would you like a free T-shirt?" I noticed there are three types of people in this world and they easily separate themselves into clear categories.

The first type of person will walk on by, paying no attention to the offer being made. Obviously, the offer is not for them or they are in a rush to get somewhere.

The second type of person will take the T-shirt and say, "Wow, thank you so much. Today is my lucky day!"

The third type of person will take the T-shirt, glance at it, and then say, "I don't like this. What else do you have, instead? I always get stuck with things I do not like." Instead of politely giving the T-shirt back, they find a reason to complain about something that was given to them as a gift!

Between the second and third type of person, who do you think will live a happier and more fulfilled life? Both have different narratives running in their lives and shaping their day.

What matters most about mindset is not as to whether you were born with it or developed it over time- the key is that you can always change your mindset. In order to do so, you must stop conditioning yourself for what you do *not* want.

You are bombarded by influences and suggestions everywhere you go. The main sources are within your repeated surroundings. What type of music do you often listen to? Who do you follow on social media? Who are your role models? Which people are around you the most? What types of books do you read or listen to? Which TV shows do you watch?

Your surroundings indirectly affect who you are, what you do, who you become and how you feel. Your surroundings have an impact on your mind, as the mind mimics what it repeatedly sees and hears.

Create Rapid Change

The most powerful and effective way to redesign your subconscious is to reframe your perspective. Your perspective is the way in which you see the world: is the glass half full or half empty? It is also known as your mindset, frame of mind and attitude.

Perspective = Power

You can positively shift your entire life within moments, simply by switching your perspective. The familiar saying rings true: When you change the way you look at things, the things you look at change.

As much as you can use the power of your subconscious mind to produce remarkable results and create a life beyond your wildest dreams, there will still be a lot that is beyond your control, despite your best efforts. The past is a prime example.

The past is the main source of suffering within your daily life because you replay the memories on a loop in your mind, as if you can fix it by doing so. The truth is, you cannot change the past, you can only alter the way you feel about the past. It is a default within the mind to dwell upon the painful memories, which will trigger a flood of negative emotions within the present.

"We all have the same potential," Dr. Natha, a Canadian physician, has observed. "If we can all learn to use our minds to their optimal level, almost anything can be done. The beliefs we have can either make us or break us."

When it comes to healing the body, mind and spirit, Dr. Natha says, "It is important to accept everything- both the good and the bad- realizing that everything that has happened to you was meant for you."

"Power is choice." Dr. Natha.

What is Your Story?

You have a huge impact on yourself through the stories you tell because they are a form of self-hypnosis. Here are examples of a few wide-spread stories that could be shaping your day:

"Bad things always happen to me. I'm always getting screwed over," vs. "Everything happens for a reason."

"It's not my fault- it's theirs," vs. "It's not my fault that it happened, but it is my responsibility to fix it."

"Why me?" vs. "Lucky me."

"Why did this have to happen now?" vs. "Good thing this happened now and not later."

A good way to find out what story is running through your head is to pay attention next time you encounter a challenge, becoming aware of the common thoughts running through your mind.

If you want to make lasting change in your life you must start re-telling your story. To do so, alter your perspective.

You have already successfully done this before.

Be honest with yourself: have you ever looked at a painting and thought it was hideous, only to find out a few moments later that it was a Picasso, worth millions of dollars? Once you learned what it was worth, you probably looked at the painting more closely, possibly even noticing the sophistication of its brushwork and the impact of its imagery.

The painting did not change- the only thing that changed was your perspective. Your perspective is the quickest and most powerful way to change your mind and your life.

So, how can you transform your perspective on purpose?

Method # 9: How to Gain Instant Power in Challenging Times

Are you ready for one of the most rapid techniques to access your mind's power and flip a situation so that you can be the champion? If this technique seems overly simple, that is because it is. However, it will be one of the best tools to transform your life.

Instructions

1. In every tough situation, develop the habit of empowering yourself by asking yourself this question: "What is the lesson or blessing in this current situation?"

Ask yourself this question every time you encounter an obstacle or challenge. You can use this while in self-hypnosis, or without being in trance. It conditions your mind to alter your perspective and become victorious- you are literally training your mind to win.

2. Find the answer. Hint: the answer is up to you. This will become one of the most dramatically life-transforming things you ever do, because if you cannot change the situation, the only thing you can change is the way you think and feel about the situation.

When you shift your attitude, wait and see how the situation will start to transform, too.

Each time Taylor Swift gets her heart broken, she turns the heartbreak into a hit song and makes millions of dollars from it.

Perspective is realizing there are several ways to use lemons- making lemonade is only one of them!

Power Now

Looking back, if I did not experience all that pain accumulating and pushing me to my limit, I would not be where I am today. The darkest hours gave me the opportunity to discover who I am, while crafting my personal power. I wish the world could experience even just a sliver of the freedom and inner peace I have discovered, and I teach people to do exactly that in my online coaching programs.

The worst times of my life were necessary in order to help me to create and appreciate the best times of my life. Life was not happening *to* me, it was happening *for* me. It all started when I became present to each moment, giving myself permission to be myself, while practicing the art of surrendering and letting go of everything else.

This is one of the hardest things to do, especially during tough times, because the ego will try to grasp at everything and attach to anything, feeling threatened by becoming nothing.

I realized that I really am nothing… and at the very same time I am everything because I am within the potential of the present.

Chapter 10
Shift Mental Patterns

Do You Sometimes Feel like there are Thoughts Stuck on Repeat?

Rest assured, that happens to everyone. Everybody experiences undesirable thoughts, feelings and days where everything seems upsetting. You will always have the highs and lows; to take that away would make you a robot- not a human.

Fortunately, there are things you can do to stop the negative fixations in your head. This will require some assessment. There are several reasons why your mind can be stuck in a negative pattern. Now is the time to address them. Here is a list of some of the things that can affect your thoughts and feelings: alcohol, drugs, medication, processed foods, sugar, a sedentary lifestyle, past traumas, sleep issues, mental/emotional/chemical/hormonal imbalances, illness, pain, food sensitivities, habits, undiagnosed issues within your mind or body, etc. Of course, there are more factors, such as, stress, anxiety, issues at work, loss and grievances, and family disturbances.

Many of the issues mentioned above will need an expert to help you correct them. If you experience thoughts of self-harm, or harming somebody else, or thoughts of suicide, seek immediate medical help. Surround yourself with a team of professionals who can help you target the root cause, while helping you to get on track.

If the thoughts stuck in your head are not compromising to your life, you will find the following steps provided below to be helpful. Below are some questions to ask yourself, so that you can help yourself become unstuck.

1. Ask yourself, "Is there a reason I am focussing on this thought so much?" Find out what the trigger was. Was it a person, a memory, something you saw or heard, etc. Sometimes your mind will daydream and run through possible scenarios when you are excited, and sometimes your mind will worry (which is another form of daydreaming) and run through the worst-case scenarios when you are upset, stressed, nervous and anxious.

Ask yourself what could be the cause? Was it something someone said? Was it an event earlier in the day? Did you see something that triggered upsetting feelings about yourself? Dig a little to find out.

2. If your mind is replaying the same negative tune, you need to address the emotions. Emotions need to be released from the mind or they will be bottled up and resurface later.

If you want to master your mind, you must be able to master your emotions.

Mastering your emotions does not mean never feeling angry or upset; it means knowing how to efficiently deal with the emotions and release them in a healthy way, and being able to switch your mood before your mood ruins your day.

If you are easily triggered by the things other people say and do- you are not in control of yourself or your emotions. It is as if you are walking around in plain sight with a big red button on your back. Of course, that button will get pushed often because it is so easily accessible.

You must learn to deal with your thoughts and emotions in a healthy way. Release them and express them- never suppress them.

3. Change your mind. Use the self-hypnosis method to put yourself into a deeper, relaxed state and then tell your mind, "Please show me what I can do in order to resolve this." Focus on the solution- not the problem. Then use your imagination to think of the things that can go right, instead of what could go wrong.

4. Change your state of being. Do something active, like twenty jumping jacks, or go for a brisk walk or punch a pillow. Making physical changes helps to initiate mental shifts.

5. Change your surroundings. Get outside and take a few deep breaths. A change of scenery can trigger changes in your mind.

Remove things from your surroundings that make you feel bad. If the music you listen to makes you emotional or angry- change it.

When you live in a cluttered and messy house, it impacts your mood, right? When you do some spring cleaning and remove the trash, you feel lighter and better, right? Do the same thing for your space- both mentally and physically.

Remove the things that are having a negative impact on your body or mind. Use self-awareness to find out what those things may be. You may even decide to do a one-week negativity cleanse, where you stop watching the news, limit your time on your phone, stop complaining, and replace those with activities that inspire you, instead.

Make sure your personal space, such as your home, is uplifting. Place a vision board where you will see it every day and use images and phrases that motivate you and make you feel pumped up. Flood your mind with positive books, audio books, music, people, affirmations and visualizations.

6. Change your perspective. Use the power of gratitude. Every single day for thirty consecutive days, physically write down five things you are grateful for. The catch? You must list something different every day- no repeating the same thing twice. Keep that list and look at it throughout the day.

7. Change your focus. Take a break. Your mind functions better when it is well-balanced. This means, scheduling time in your day where you can do something that makes you feel happy. Google headquarters has provided their employees with things like ping pong tables and nap pods because research shows that switching your focus for a time can help increase your productivity.

8. Speak to someone. Know when you need a medical expert vs. when you need a friend to help snap you out of it vs. when you just need someone to make you feel seen, heard and give you a sense of belonging.

9. If the body is not well, the mind will not be well. Health, peace and happiness come from taking care of your body and mind.

What Do You Do About Negative People?

Avoid them as much as possible. Negative people are stuck in their own ways, inflicting misery onto everyone else because they are hurting and unhappy with themselves. They would much rather blame others for their misery and complain about everything, because they are under the illusion that doing those two things makes them look better than others.

The world can see through that BS. Insecure people whine and complain about others, while confident and self-secure people uplift, compliment and help others. Negative people will always find a reason to complain or attack you, because there is something about you that causes them to self-reflect and they do not like what they see in the mirror. Therefore, they attack you because it is their way of ignoring the ugly feelings within themselves.

Have standards for yourself, including the type of people you invest your time with. Life is short, and you can never regain wasted time. The quality of my friends improved dramatically once I decided to have great friends. This, in turn, affects happiness, because we are all extremely happy every time that we get together.

You become like the people you hang around because your mind is constantly picking up on your surroundings on an unconscious level. If you want to pick up subliminal motivation, inspiration, possibilities and confidence in your abilities, hang out with people who are already where you want to be. If there are thought leaders you admire, follow them online. These days many of those leaders are posting content throughout the day, and the more of their content you seek, the more it will sink into your mind.

Part of creating happiness for yourself comes from removing the things that no longer make you happy and surrounding yourself with the things that bring you true joy.

How to Win Around a Negative Person without Taking the Lower Ground

Simply be happy and succeed at your goals. Nothing annoys them more. Plus, this way you are taking the higher road, instead of sinking to their level.

Realistically, you cannot avoid every negative person, because, unfortunately, some of them will be in your family or workplace. You cannot change anyone- it is up to them to change themselves. You can unlock the door of the prison they are living in, and show them that the door is wide open, but, it is up to them to leave the prison.

Unfortunately, you cannot control what other people think about you. You can control how you react to them and how long you allow their drama to affect you. Keep your focus on the one thing you can control: yourself.

Hypnotists' Secret # 8
The Power of Triggering Emotions

Being that the subconscious mind is the feeling mind, a fast way to access it is through emotion. This can be done through telling stories.

Several TV shows use this secret in order to hook the viewer in and keep their attention. Think of the popular singing competition shows. They introduce a contestant, tell their backstory about how something tragic happened to them and how they turned their life around and now they are on the show, hoping for the chance of a lifetime to completely transform their life and turn it around. It is known as the American Dream- the hope of going from nothing to something, from rags to riches. When you can relate to someone, you pay more attention to them and root them on, giving them more of your focus.

Your power flows in the same direction as your focus.

Chapter 11
eMOTIONS

It is human nature to label everything and attach meaning to it all. We are obsessed with categorizing everything as either good or bad. When we are feeling happy, we call it good and when we are feeling sad, we call it bad. When we do this we create a whole load of issues. Every time we feel a "bad" emotion, such as guilt, frustration, anger or depression, we create more of that emotion.

When you were younger, there were a few times when you were crying and then a parent figure came along and said, "Stop crying." The same thing happened when you were angry; you were told, "Stop being angry." Now, as an adult, any time you start crying, you hear the voice in your head telling you to stop crying and stop being mad.

As much as your parents meant well, this process taught you to suppress certain emotions, feeling upset with yourself each time you feel guilty, angry, sad, frustrated and depressed. That voice that you are hearing is the voice of that parent figure, which became your programming, triggered by something within your current circumstances. You often follow that voice, mistaking it as your own.

While continuing to work on improving the quality of your thoughts, words and actions, there are a few more simple and effective ways to create more joy for yourself.

Method # 10: How to Create More Emotional Balance
1. Remove the Labels

The first thing to do is to stop labeling your emotions as either good or bad. They are simply either preferable or non-preferable; comfortable or uncomfortable; positive or negative. When you are driving your car and the dashboard indicator lights up telling you that you are low on fuel, do you get mad at your car and start exclaiming, "This is bad. It shouldn't be this way. What is wrong with this vehicle! Why does it always need gas?" The fact is, your car needs gas. That is neither good nor bad. An empty tank of gas does not mean the car is broken or that it needs to be fixed.

You will encounter challenges. You will face tough situations. You will have times where you feel unwanted emotions, such as depression. So just because you experience low times, it does not mean there is something wrong with you. It means you are a human being, designed to feel a range of feelings and that you are still alive. Stop making yourself feel bad or wrong for feeling a variety of emotions.

There will be things that are outside of your control, despite your best efforts. However, you have the power within you to help yourself get through the tough days and come out on top as an improved version of yourself.

Remember, there is a time for everything. The range in your emotions adds contrast to your life. If you were happy all the time, would you even know you were happy? Would you appreciate the highs without experiencing the lows?

2. Acknowledge Your Feelings

If you are driving to work and somebody cuts you off, causing you to swerve, you have the right to be angry. However, you do not have the right to take that anger out on anybody, including yourself.

Let yourself feel your emotions (for a few moments, *not* all day- there is a vast difference!) When you feel an unwanted feeling, such as anger, take some time to acknowledge it. Doing so can make most unwanted emotions disappear within moments. Simply, take a few deep breaths while telling yourself, "I have the right to feel this feeling." Repeat that for a few minutes while observing the location in your body where you feel that emotion. There is no need to even label the feeling "anger" as doing so can create more of that feeling through the power of suggestion (your words).

After breathing deeply and letting yourself feel the emotion, you will notice the emotion has either diminished or disappeared altogether. This is a daily practice, so be patient with yourself. Just because you are taking the time to work on personal development or to heal the past does not mean that you will never feel uncomfortable feelings again. You are a human being- not a robot.

You have a right to your feelings, just make sure you deal with them appropriately. Fighting them or supressing them will only cause them to persist.

3. Express Yourself

Your body is your vehicle for your time here on Earth. You will need to deal with situations such as hunger, thirst, tiredness and a bunch of different feelings. Just like the different lights on your car's dashboard indicate what is happening within the car, your emotions are indicators as to what is going on within you.

Nobody wants to go get their oil changed, but when the light comes on, you know it is important for your vehicle to operate at its best and it helps to prevent damage down the road. Nobody wants to experience pain or sadness or loneliness. However, you will have periods of time in your life where you experience those things and possibly more or less. You must find a way to express the emotions and deal with them.

If you still feel the emotion after following step number two above, then do something active to dissolve the emotion, such as going for a walk or exercising at the gym. Some people also find it extremely insightful to keep a journal and let their feelings flow onto the pages.

4. Switch Focus

Instead of waking up in the morning and saying things like, "I hope today isn't going to be a bad day," or "I don't want to feel sad today," suggest to yourself *what you want*. Say something like, "Today is going to be one of the best days of my life."

Choose to focus on the positive. Choose to find the silver lining. Hypnotize yourself to believe that good things are heading your way.

5. Socialize

We are social beings and are intended to be in groups. Social media and technology has taken away the need to meet up with people in person. As a result, we have drawn away from each other and are lonelier than ever. Go out with a group of friends or at the very least, talk to a friend via video chat. Do something to socialize and connect with other people.

6. Do You

Trying to please everyone is the shortcut to a miserable life. At some point you have to realize what your boundaries are and you have to start putting your happiness and well-being above others. Stop valuing the opinion of people who do not value you. Stand up for yourself, instead of waiting for others to do it. Everybody is busy in their own minds doing whatever it takes just to make themselves feel good- we are all in that same boat.

Do something to mend your soul and make it sing, while being a kind person. You can do *both*- it is not a one or the other scenario.

7. Have Fun!

In this example, pretend you have a puppy. She is a cute little furry thing with tons of excitement and energy. Can you imagine what would happen if you took her home, locked her in a room, and ignored her for a few hours or even days? She would have chewed up everything she could sink her teeth into, made a mess everywhere, and be malnourished due to long periods of thirst and hunger. If you want that puppy to stay healthy and happy, you must take care of her needs, right?

Treat your mind like a puppy. Your mind needs positive attention, fun and nourishment. Train your mind, instead of your mind training you. Learn from your emotions, feel them and then move on. Do something fun. Give yourself reasons to be happy or the mind will naturally find reasons to be unhappy over time. This should be common sense: your mind functions optimally and feels its best when you are having fun. If you have stopped taking the time to have fun, how can you expect your mind to be happy? Balance is key.

Happiness must be cultivated every single day through your thoughts, words and actions. Take at least twenty minutes per day to do something you enjoy. This can even mean listening to an audiobook on the way to work, creating a picture in an adult coloring book, singing in the shower, cuddling your lover while watching Netflix, going for a walk outdoors on your lunch break, grabbing a coffee with a friend, or listening to your favorite upbeat music. Create balance within your day, even if that means scheduling it in.

We are all bound to have highs and lows in life. The saddest and toughest days were the times when I learned some of the greatest lessons of my life. My life is more meaningful now than it ever was before.

I am not happy because I have no problems. I set myself up for happiness by focussing on the things that are going right, instead of the things that are going wrong.

5 Ways to Increase Your Happiness Today
Practice Daily Happiness

Too many of us wait for happiness to happen to us or we attach it to external things and achievements. When we do this, happiness is short-lived and out of our control because it is dependent upon external circumstances, rendering us powerless. A powerful person is someone who realizes there will be ups and downs in their journey, however, they have found the tools to be happy despite the highs and lows. Happiness is like the sun: it is always present above the clouds. Sometimes we must rise above the clouds in order to experience it.

1. Develop an Attitude of Gratitude

a. Sit in a safe and comfortable position with your eyes closed.

b. Focus on something you are grateful for. Picture it in detail, bringing your awareness to how good you feel.

c. Imagine that you can intensify that good feeling within yourself and visualize it spreading throughout your body, until it overflows.

When you are in a state of love and gratitude, you are tuned in to a higher frequency. This is the state where you are most able to control your mind, experience your potential, feel profound happiness and use your power to create the abundantly satisfying life you truly want.

To get your day off to the best start, take a few moments to focus on the feeling of gratitude.

When you think of the *things* you are grateful for, you are *activating* your internal power; when you focus on the *feeling* of gratitude, you are *amplifying* your internal power.

You already know how to do this, as it is something the mind naturally does during times where you feel stressed, ill or in pain. The mind will focus on the negative feeling and you repeat it in your head, thinking, "Uh, I feel so stressed."

Yet, the mind does not always naturally do this when you feel something positive. It is up to you to get yourself in the habit of noticing when you feel good and focussing your mind to expand up on it.

The power of gratitude shifts your attitude.

2. Switch to Happiness Mode

Your physical stance can create negative feelings or powerful ones. Have you noticed how depressed people usually have a slumped over posture while confident people have their shoulders back? Control your stance to control your mood.

a. Stand tall with your feet shoulder width apart and place your hands on your hips.

b. Pull your shoulders back, raise your chin, and look forward above eye level.

c. While maintaining this stance, bring a smile to your face, breathing deeply for 3-5 minutes.

3. Commit a Random Act of Kindness

Studies show that the people who are happiest in their lives are the ones who find a way to give back to society and serve others. One of the best things you can do is to donate your time to those who are in need, because it will expand your mind, get you outside of your head and help you to change your perspective. Being around others who have fewer things and bigger problems creates gratitude and appreciation within your life, which will help you to experience more wealth and happiness.

4. Create Purpose

Research shows that the healthiest and happiest people are the ones who have created a sense of purpose for themselves. Find a reason to get out of bed in the morning and set goals on a regular basis throughout your life.

5. Stay in Connection with Community

Join a group of like-minded people. Avoid isolating yourself, as that often has a negative impact on the mind.

6. Give Yourself Something to Look Forward to

Set a goal with a specific date or book a vacation. Give your mind a reason to be happy and a timeline so that you have something to focus on, where the date is approaching, no matter what. Avoid pushing the date back to prevent procrastination.

"Be happy with whatever life you have. Appreciate all of the goodness in the world. Power comes from the faith that you are on the right path. If you have faith, you have power." Kelley Schedewitz, Hair Stylist in Vancouver, B.C. www.loveyourhair.ca

Chapter 12
Boost Your Motivation

Motivation is killed by fear, which can manifest in so many ways: fear of failure, fear of what other people think, fear of rejection, fear of pain, fear of humiliation, and fear of loss. This all comes down to the primitive nature of the subconscious mind which wants to keep you safe within the confines of your comfort zone, sticking to what is familiar.

Even though you may dislike your current situation, it is at least known to you and therefore provides a certain level of comfort.

When your mind finds a solution that works, it will apply it repeatedly in multiple areas of your life, causing a ripple effect. To your subconscious, a solution could mean either eating junk food when you are stressed, drinking excessively or prodding yourself to the gym. One of those solutions will become a default coping mechanism for you when you repeat it. This is either programmed behaviour you picked up from the authority figures in your life or learned behaviour you have repetitively conditioned yourself with over the years.

Positive changes can snowball with a ripple effect in a beneficial way. The more you practice discipline and train your mind, the more you improve, the more you will notice other areas of your life improving, as well. You can call this the Law of Attraction or simply a law of the subconscious.

When you pull the weeds, you will immediately see more natural beauty in the garden. Your subconscious "cross-pollinates" whatever you plant and nurture in the garden of your mind: flowers or weeds.

You are breaking old habits and forming new ones. This is why people often say, "it gets harder before it gets easier." Once you create a positive habit, it becomes second nature to you.

Fear is an illusion of the mind that has been conditioned throughout your life. The more you talk about fear and the more you dwell upon it, the more fear you will experience, because your mind will expand on it.

Be aware of your mind becoming addicted to being fearful or talking about the things you fear. If you find you like the attention you get when you tell others about the things that scare you, you will only make it more challenging for yourself to get over it.

Remember, your words and stories are self-hypnosis, conditioning you.

Fear can be handed down through generations of family members from programming or it can be a learned response to an event you experienced. All fear can be overcome. The best way to do that is to confront it, which will help to desensitize you from it.

Focus on what it will feel like to have triumphed over the things that frighten you. Think about the freedom and sense of accomplishment you will have.

Below are two methods often used in Hypnotherapy to help produce dramatic results. You can use these methods without a deep state of hypnosis. They become most powerful when you exercise them daily, until it becomes an unconscious way of being.

You are what You Repeat

You may be familiar with the saying, "You are what you repeatedly do." You are also what you repetitiously think and feel. This is a form of conditioning yourself.

If every morning on your way to work, you tell yourself how much you hate your job, what are you programming your mind for? How can you expect to arrive at work one day and love it if you are conditioning yourself to subconsciously focus on all the reasons you are unhappy with your current situation?

This applies to all areas of your life. When you repeatedly combine a thought plus an emotion plus an action, you are programming your mind for a certain experience.

You shape your perspective and form your reality on autopilot through the power of habit.

Redesign your life by shifting your perspective. Below are a few simple and effective examples of how you can begin to reframe your perspective:

Start your day by listing the many blessings you have instead of the things you feel you are lacking.

Concentrate on the things that are going right for you, instead of the problem areas.

Instead of telling yourself, "This is ruining my life," switch it to, "This is pushing me towards something better."

Focus on all of the people who are succeeding in your line of business as opposed to failing.

Notice the random acts of kindness happening around you instead of the crime.

Switch your mindset to faith, possibilities and solutions instead of fear, worries and problems.

Focus on the things that make you happy instead of the things that make you sad.

Think of ways you can give to others instead of thinking of what you can get from others.

Connect to something larger than yourself, such as a greater purpose or a higher power, instead of focussing on all the little things and trying to do everything yourself.

Switch your awareness to the things you can change and let go of the things you cannot change.

If you hate your job and you are unwilling or unable to find a new one, then you must switch your thinking and the way you feel about it.

If your relationship is going through rocky times, find ways to improve yourself instead of focussing on the weaknesses your partner may have.

Retrain Your Subconscious and Reprogram the Present

Love your life and things will get better instead of waiting for things to get better before you love your life.

You create bigger problems for yourself by thinking you should not have any problems. You create negative feelings for yourself by thinking with a negative frame of mind.

What is the common theme here? Your outlook. Everyone has problems; however, some people have trained themselves to be better at dealing with them.

Your repeated thoughts, words, actions and habits are hypnotic to your subconscious. What type of suggestions are you giving yourself?

7 Reasons Tough Times are Beneficial for You:

1. They Show You Who is Really There for You

It is easy for people to like you when things are going well. However, it is far better to know which of those people truly care about you, especially when you are at your lowest.

2. They Make You Stronger

If you want to get stronger physically, you must exercise and lift weights. Each time you lift the weight it creates tiny tears in your muscles. When the muscle repairs them, it becomes stronger and larger than it was before.

Professional bodybuilders come to love the feeling of pushing their bodies "to failure" or to the point where they feel so exhausted that they cannot lift any more weight. These physical challenges are needed in order to create physical strength.

In a similar way, your mind becomes stronger when you face the tough and challenging times of life. If you never challenge yourself, you will never know how strong you really are.

3. They Add Contrast into Your Life

Just as contrast is necessary for your eyes to see everything properly, the highs and lows have their purpose in your life, too.

Without darkness, would you be able to see the stars?

Without sadness, would you know when you were happy?

4. They Give You the Opportunity to Grow and Evolve

Challenges are opportunities to stop, adjust and innovate, often causing you to change your ways of thinking, acting and being in order to create the desired outcome.

Without obstacles, would you take the time for self-improvement?

5. They Nudge You Down a Better Path

When you look at each challenge or failure as a lesson and you become innovative, you alter your thoughts, actions and behaviours, therefore, creating entirely new results. When your mindset is in the right place, tough times will nudge you in the right direction, pushing you towards something greater.

6. They Build Confidence and Courage

The only time you can be brave is while you are still afraid.

While doing new things and overcoming things that used to break you down you will find a new-found sense of solid confidence growing.

7. They Teach You Appreciation

They help you to recognize and value the things that matter the most to you, giving you the chance to experience more gratitude, happiness, satisfaction and power.

What you appreciate appreciates.

Method # 11: How to Start Your Day off as Your Most Powerful Self

Condition yourself to be your best by starting out the day with these two suggestions:

"Something wonderful is about to happen."

"I choose to be the best version of myself and make today the best day of my life."

PILLAR 3
CREATE

Chapter 13
Life is like a Game of Poker

In 2017 Bryn Kenney won the highest amount of money of any poker player in one year: $8.5 million. What most people do not know is that the previous year was his worst year ever, with a debt of $2.5 million.

So, how did he go from his worst year, with millions of dollars down the drain, to becoming arguably the best poker player of 2017? Most people would have just thrown in the towel after losing so much money. But Bryn is not like most people.

Just as life can take a drastic turn for the worse, so can a game of poker, as Bryn's experience demonstrates. He was ripped off in a bad business deal and he watched some of the people he considered friends turn a cold shoulder to him, even though he had been there to help them out during their own dark times. "People act very different to you when you're winning and when you're losing," Bryn comments. "When things are good, everyone is your best friend and when things are bad, no one knows your name anymore."

Bryn gave himself one week to move past his lowest low. He locked himself in a tiny apartment in London, turned his phone off, and told himself that only he was responsible for his fate, so all he could do was to take baby steps to get himself out of it.

Less than one month later, Bryn won $1.5 million in a big tournament in Manila, Philippines. Ironically, his poker face was so opaque, nobody could have known anything was wrong with him at the time. He says, "When you're playing a gambling game, you don't want people to know when you're down because they will try to go after you." Bryn went on to have the highest winning year of all time in poker. Besides earning millions of dollars throughout his career, Bryn has developed many valuable insights along the way, which can be applied to succeeding in any area of life.

Successfully Playing the Game of Life:
8 Life-Changing Insights from the World's Greatest Poker Player

1. Develop Mental Strength

"When people ask me what the most important thing in poker is," Bryn tells me, "I always answer, Mental Strength. Same thing in life; it is all just like a poker game. It is much harder to make good decisions than it is to make mistakes. People get tested when they're at their lowest- and I'm like a gladiator. I always saw it like I can't quit because if I quit, not only do I give up on myself, but I give up on all the people closest to me that I can help out if things are going well for me. It's never in my head that you can actually give up." In tough times, look at the facts. Then ask yourself what you can do to create the best outcome for your future. Understand it will take time and effort to get there.

2. Stay Calm

Bryn observes, "Poker is the game where there are a lot of up and down swings, so if you're letting yourself be affected on either side- either when you go up or when you go down, it's just going to be much tougher for you." The same can be said about life.

Bryn's mental strength and positive outlook are something he developed over time, realizing the importance of remaining calm throughout the ups and downs of both his career and life.

"Complaining and negativity are never going to bring you back to where you want to be," he offers. "You'll just be stuck in that hole forever."

3. Stay Sharp

Bryn keeps his mind sharp by getting a good night's rest, drinking lots of water and being mindful to avoid foods that can weigh him down physically and mentally. He also avoids allowing events of the past to affect him by forgetting about the past completely.

4. Create Balance

Playing an average of 10-12 hours every day since he was 17, the now 31-year-old Bryn realizes that balance is the most important thing in life. While money used to be the central focal point for him, Bryn learned from several smart, wealthy, older people who told him that if they could change anything, they wouldn't work their whole life. Wisely, Bryn says, "It's not really about money, its more about experiences. Money dies with you."

Take time for yourself. Go on a vacation, turn your phone off. Ignore any type of outside noise and just allow your mind to process.

5. Build Your Own Confidence.

In both poker and life, you will do better when you are confident within yourself. Bryn claims he was the most hated person in his high school because of the way he dressed. He would tell himself,

"Who cares what these idiots think. They're going to be in the same town for their whole life and they're just going to be googling my name and seeing it somewhere else. So forget about these guys."

Genuine and lasting confidence is not something that is handed to you. It comes from building it and earning it for yourself. "When you are confident in yourself and you work hard, then you can get anything you want," Bryn claims. "People will feel that confidence. People will also hate you for the confidence that you have, but you can't let that bring you down."

6. Detach from what Others Think

Listen to your close friends if they give you constructive criticism. Other than that, detach from what other people have to say about you. "As you start to build more," Bryn advises, "the outside noise becomes louder and louder. For me, who cares about what other people who don't know you have to think. If they want to hate on you that's just because they're sitting in their basement doing nothing."

When you have made substantial positive improvements in your life and people tell you, "You've changed," it's usually because they are comparing your life to theirs, which makes them feel insecure and jealous. The brighter you glow, the more people in the shade will start to glare. Shine bright anyways- it's their job to adjust their own focus.

7. Work Hard

Be easier on yourself. There are going to be tough times. You are going to be tested along the way. Take baby steps. As Bryn says, "See, a lot of people think that you can try to jump a mountain- just run up the mountain as fast as possible. You've got to take baby steps just to be somewhere on that mountain.

"Learn from the past, make better decisions, and do what you can in order to make improvements. It is possible to fail while putting in the right effort. If you believe you are on the right path, but the results aren't coming, that's just because there are some variants involved, and the results will come, as long you keep making the proper effort. If you work hard, and do the right thing, then good things will come to you without a doubt."

8. Change Your Perspective.

Instead of being bothered by results, focus on the effort you put in. Take a step back and look at things from a different standpoint. Typically, people feel their weakest when they are at their lowest point; however, when he is at his worst, Bryn becomes more ferocious.

"Power is the ability to do what you want and to be able to give the same to the people that you care about," Bryn says.

To succeed in both poker and life, it's all about mindset. Whether you are born with it or not, you must learn to develop a positive and strong mindset on your journey.

Chapter 14
Create a New Internal Belief System

Welcome to the third pillar!

The Benefits of Pillar 3: Create
- Replace unwanted patterns with healthy patterns
- Visualize effectively
- Manifest the things you want
- Redesign specific areas of your mind or character
- Become the person you have always wanted to be
- Boost happiness, self-confidence, self-certainty, self-belief, and self-worth
- Give yourself the tools to be your most kickass self
- Program your mind with a "Happiness Button"

In pillar three, you will learn effective methods to create:
1. A New Internal Belief System
2. A New Reality

Are you ready to start discovering how much power you have? Are you ready to allow yourself to find out what you are capable of creating and achieving?

Before I teach you how to create what you want, there are a few things you should know.

Will the Results be Permanent?

Imagine you live in a house that was built a few years ago. The framework is still in good condition, but the interior is outdated, shabby and rundown. Plus, it is not up to your style standards. You hired a team of experts, did some renovations, clearing out the things that you did not want and now you have your dream home in place.

Will that house stay clean, modern, up to date and stylish? That is up to you. It is better to stay on top of things and do regular maintenance, keeping an eye on everything, updating as you go, instead of waiting until another major renovation is required.

By the end of this book, you will have the techniques and ability to connect to your subconscious mind, clear away the limiting internal programming and create more of what you want.

These are tools you can use for the rest of your life- and you will obviously need to continue to use them for the rest of your life. Can you begin to imagine how much you can positively alter your life and succeed?

Remember, if you are taking the time to correctly program your mind, your new skills will become habits, automating and working for you on autopilot. They will get easier, more natural and more effective as you continue to use them. Are you ready to amplify your power and accelerate the process even more?

Hypnotists' Secret # 9: The Power of Your Imagination

The best way to tap into your imagination is to use metaphors and similes. This is a form of indirect suggestion that has a strong impact on the subconscious mind, which is the feeling mind. It helps the mind to produce specific experiences and results by providing the mind with an example of what to do. The mind has an easier time to create something that is already known to it, as opposed to inventing something entirely different on the spot.

Imagine I was hypnotizing you and I told you, "Jump up and down." Let's say that you followed my instructions and jumped up and down.

Now, say I gave you the suggestion, "Jump up and down as if you just found out you won the lottery- a jackpot worth $300 million!"

> I bet you would be jumping up and down in a way that looks completely different the previous because now your mind has a mental image of what to do and how to do it.
> Plus, the second suggestion changed your entire mood, with the flip of a switch. Am I right?

Use Your Dreams to Create Your Dreams

Have you ever become so caught up in a daydream, that you lost track of what was happening around you, including the time? Your subconscious mind does not know the difference between reality and the imagination.

What I mean by this is, the subconscious mind feels everything to some degree and the more emotion, focus or repetition involved, the more real it becomes to the subconscious mind. You know when you are watching a scary movie, your heartrate is beginning to speed up. You start to feel anxiety spreading through your body, as your inner voice is screaming at the main character, "Get out of there!"

Consciously, you know everything in the movies is staged, including the character, but deep down you are still caught up in the moment, and even though you know it's coming, you still jump at the frightening scene.

The good news is, you have been using this incredible key to access your subconscious since you were a child.

The bad news is, this power most often gets misused and abused, which ends up creating more of what you do not what.

Do you ever find yourself caught up, worrying about something bad that could go wrong, and then you begin to feel the signs of stress in the pit of your stomach, or you catch yourself holding your breath?

Worry is a misuse of the power of your subconscious mind. The more you use your imagination to picture the negative outcomes, the more you are programming yourself to become negative. It hinders creativity, happiness, the ability to solve problems, and your own personal power.

It is a well-known fact that many professional athletes use visualization before the game as a way of improving their performance. There is a lot of science behind it. Visualization is a powerful technique to train your subconscious mind to help you to achieve what you want and it works best when you use mental pictures combined with emotion.

"If you want to be successful at something," says Tommy Europe, actor and former CFL player, "you have to see yourself being successful. That opens different doors to your mind so that when setbacks do happen or when things don't go the way you think they're going to go, it doesn't deter you from your ultimate goal because you've seen yourself succeed at it."

Tommy would know- his dreams of being in the NFL came crashing down. Being an athlete gave him a thick skin, and he knew he was tough, so, Tommy did not let this challenge set him back. He continued working on himself and visualizing the life he wanted.

He ended up moving to a new city after being drafted into the CFL and that is where he met his wife. Although things may not have worked out exactly how he initially wanted, he wound up getting something even better.

"Visualization works," claims Tommy. He has since had his own T.V. shows and started his own fitness boot camp to help people reach their health and fitness goals. "Visualization is something everybody should incorporate into their lives- not just athletes."

"Power is being on top of your game, physically, mentally, socially- all aspects. SHRED: Strength, Heart, Resilience, Efficiency, Discipline. That's my power. Over the years, if you apply this to all areas of your life or goals, you're going to be successful in reaching your goal," Tommy.

Imagination is the magical key to accessing the subconscious mind. If you continue to see yourself as the same old person, you will continue to have the same old problems and the same old results. To create a new internal belief system, you must have a new vision. It is crucial to see yourself differently within your mind. Not only does that train your mind to think of yourself in a new way, it places your focus on being who you want to be instead of being where you are.

With your mind focussed on the new version of you, your mind will become aware of new opportunities to help you get to where you want to be. Think of it as creating muscle memory. Although you are not at your goal yet, you are conditioning your mind to be familiar with attaining your goal. When you can perform skillsets naturally, you do them with confidence. The more you repeat scenarios in your mind, the more familiar they become to your mind.

Which scenarios are you repeating to yourself: worst case or best case?

Visualization = The Power of Focus + The Power of Awareness + The Power of Imagination + The Power of Perspective. All working together at the same time!

Method # 12: Visualizing and Manifesting what You Want

Learn how to make visualization the most effective for you. Manifesting starts within your mind. It is important to note, it is not your thoughts alone that will change your life. Your thoughts can change your feelings, which change your behaviours, which change your actions, in turn, producing new outcomes.

Celebrities and athletes use visualization to make their dreams come true and so should you. First, you must know what you want and why you want it. This has to do with the Law of Awareness: your mind expands upon the things you focus on.

Write your goal down and keep it where you will see it often.

Seeing imaginatively is a natural language of the subconscious mind; you can use this to make visualization work better for you.

Instructions*

1. Sit down in a safe and comfortable position and close your eyes. Use the self-hypnosis method previously mentioned- and once you have gotten to the bottom of the stairs and opened the treasure chest, proceed to the following instructions.

2. Pretend your mind has a movie theatre within it and imagine that you can fast forward into the future, to a time when

you have already reached your goals. Focus on the details of that experience.

How do you look? What thoughts are going through your head? What expression is on your face? How are you carrying yourself? How do other people speak about you or to you? What new healthy habits do you have?

3. This is the most important step! Picture yourself already at your goal, as if it is in the present moment and attach emotion to it. You must shift the current state of your body and convince yourself to feel as though you are in that future moment, as if it is happening now.

In your imagination, now that you have reached your goal, how do you feel about it? Focus on that good feeling and amplify it as much as possible.

Visualization is the most powerful when you pair it with *sensations*.

4. If your future self could have a conversation with you about reaching your goals, what would it say to you? What advice would it give you?

5. Once you have felt a shift in the way you feel, bring your awareness back into the present moment, bringing the uplifting sensations and wisdom with you and use the self-hypnosis method to exit hypnosis, ascending the stairs.

6. Make those new ways of being your current reality, acting as if there is no difference between you and that future version of yourself. This is a great way to condition yourself to do what it takes to make your dreams come true.

Use this process before every event, meeting and presentation. In fact, this method is a great way to start the day and set your intentions for what you want.

By convincing your mind that you are already at your goal, and acting as if that is the current reality, you are programming your mind to change your behaviours and become that successful person now.

Chapter 15
Create a New Reality

Your new reality starts now, within this present moment, and it is created by transforming the way you feel, think, act, and perceive the world around you.

Focus on changing your feelings. When you can change the way you feel, you can change your reality. A new reality presents brand new possibilities and new results.

You can alter your feelings at any moment by renewing your thinking, actions and perceptions using any of the methods provided within this book. Are you beginning to see how much control you have?

Every moment brings with it the opportunity to renew yourself and recreate yourself to be who you want to be. Every moment gives you the chance to enter a new reality.

Create What You Want on Autopilot

Each time you indulge in a habit, your mind is on autopilot-meaning, there is little to no conscious thoughts or efforts involved. This happens when you have done a task several times before, so now you do it without thinking about it.

The more you do something, the more comfortable and familiar your mind becomes with the behavior, and in turn the more likely your mind is to turn this into a habit. Remember, the subconscious mind likes to do what is familiar and comfortable.

This is something that you can use to your advantage. First, get out your journal and follow these instructions:

1. Make a list of the habits that you would like to install into your subconscious mind.
2. Choose the one that is the most important to you.

3. Make a list of the habits that you would like to uninstall from your subconscious mind. Which behaviours, thought patterns or characteristics are preventing you from reaching your goals?

Once you have your answers, proceed to the following method.

Method # 13: Uninstalling old Patterns and Installing New Ones

Create a new way of being.
Instructions*

1. Choose ONE unwanted pattern that you want to *uninstall* from your subconscious mind and ONE wanted pattern that you want to *install* into your subconscious.

2. In a safe and comfortable position, follow the self-hypnosis method, and imagine yourself opening the treasure chest.

3. Imagine that you can rewind the movie in your mind, and go back to the most recent time you experienced that particular unwanted pattern. Picture that memory in detail and make note of how you feel.

4. Find the reason why your mind installed that unwanted pattern. The subconscious mind will have kept it there because it fulfills a need for you on some level. It either avoids some form of pain, or provides you with some form of pleasure.

For example: Laura eats healthy all day at work. Then she gets home, sits down in front of the TV and consumes a large bowl of ice cream, followed by a bag of potato chips. When she was in a deep trance, she asked her mind what purpose that late night bingeing served her. Her mind told her it was her way of coping with all of the stress from the day, numbing her mind, and making her feel better. Her mind was trying to help her get away from the pain and move towards pleasure.

5. Ask your mind, "What can I do, instead, to produce those same feelings?" It is important to replace one pattern with another, otherwise it will be very difficult to make the new behaviour stick.

As strange as this may sound, do some mental bartering with your subconscious until you come up with a healthier behaviour that will provide your unconscious mind with the same feeling.

Example: Laura's mind wanted to come home and eat a healthy meal that she has already prepared earlier that week and then go for a walk.

6. Ask your mind, "How does _____ (unwanted pattern) really make me feel?" Analyze how you feel an hour later, the following day, week, and month.

When I used to binge on junk-food, there was nothing worse than how I felt afterwards. My stomach would hurt, my skin would break out like crazy, and I would feel gross. Plus, I felt angry, guilty, disappointed and ashamed that I had let this happen again, because it prevented me from reaching my goals of feeling great- both mentally and physically.

Really focus on the negative effects that the unwanted pattern causes you to experience. What feelings do you feel? What thoughts come up?

Do you see how much that unwanted pattern is holding you back from all the happiness and success that you want? Are you ready to put an end to all of that self-inflicted torment? Are you ready to let yourself succeed now?

7. Repeat it in your mind, using this formula, "_____ (unwanted pattern) causes _____ (form of pain or suffering). I am done with that. I choose to _____ (new pattern) instead, because it makes me feel ____ (good feeling, reward)."

Example: "Bingeing on junk food causes me to feel horrible, mentally and physically. It makes my stomach hurt, it lowers my confidence, and causes me to gain weight and no longer fit into my clothes. I am now done with that. I choose to take care of myself by eating healthy and exercising instead, because it makes me feel accomplished, happy, proud of myself, healthy, confident and energetic."

Be as specific as you can. Repeat that formula in your head ten times, and bring up as much emotion as you can. Really feel the pleasure as opposed to the pain.

8. In the movie theatre of your mind, fast forward to a time when the outdated pattern would have been used (example, Laura would fast forward to coming home from work after a long, stressful day).

Picture yourself acting out the new pattern instead of the old one. How does this new pattern make you feel? Do you notice how proud of yourself you feel? Focus on those good feelings and see this future self as your current self- like it is an automatic update!

9. Tell yourself, "These updates are now permanent within my subconscious mind and they will take place immediately."

10. Count yourself up the stairs and out of trance, bringing with you the new positive feelings.

Obviously, it will be much stronger and more effective when you have a hypnotherapist walk you through the above mentioned technique, usually creating results within a couple of sessions. My clients start to notice impressive results right away.

If you are doing this on your own, be patient. You are learning a new skill and this process may need to be repeated several days in a row before it takes effect. Also, keep in mind you are reprogramming your mind and body- rewiring old habits that have been in place for a long time. It is important to stay consistent and persistent.

If you accidently slip into an old pattern, catch yourself right away and say to yourself, "No, this makes me feel ____ (form of pain.) I am doing ____ (new pattern) instead, because it makes me feel ____ (new positive feeling)."

Forgive yourself for the mistake and start over in that moment. The mind will try to give you an easy out and say you will start over tomorrow. This is procrastination.

Break free of procrastination by starting again *right now*- no excuses.

> ## Hypnotists' Secret # 10:
> ## The Power of Confidence
>
> Hypnotists are confident of their skills and abilities, giving them more authority when they are performing. Authority is necessary for suggestions to be effective.
>
> Hypnosis is a numbers game. If a hypnotist gets annoyed each time someone does not go into a deep state of hypnosis, their confidence will become compromised and they will lose their sense of authority. Instead, hypnotists know that they will "fail" at getting the desired results from everybody, especially in a short amount of time. If you are in sales, you understand that it is a similar situation.
>
> When volunteers come onstage, hypnotists expect that some people will not be entertaining, some will resist, some will not understand what to do, some will be scared, and some will be already putting themselves into a trance because of how excited they are and how much they believe in it. The larger the audience, the higher are the odds that more people will be entertaining on the stage.

Choose Confidence

People always ask me how I am so confident. In reality, it comes down to this: what other choice do I have? Being insecure sucks and feels terrible. Admittedly, I do experience times of insecurity and self-doubt. I feel it for a few moments and then I decide to move out of my head and into the present moment.

Your inner thoughts will resonate through your face, voice and actions. Your level of confidence is evident to others on both a conscious and unconscious level.

Keep this in mind: confidence is like any other feeling, such as happiness, courage, inner peace, sadness or anger- they come and go like the waves of the ocean. You cannot prevent yourself from feeling one or the other. A wave is a *part* of the ocean- not the whole ocean. It is continuously moving.

You are the ocean- not the wave.

Practice daily confidence and happiness. Confidence comes from continuing to step into your best self and from being present in the moment. Confidence is not a lack of flaws, it is the ability to be yourself, despite having flaws- and acknowledging them. Confidence begins with being real and authentic with people, including yourself.

Chapter 16
Create Triggers and Buttons

Method # 14: Posthypnotic Suggestion

A posthypnotic suggestion is an instruction that is given to you while you are in trance, with the intention that you will still feel its effects after coming out of hypnosis. How long will this suggestion have a lasting effect? That all depends on the suggestion given and how often the hypnotized person acts on that suggestion.

Posthypnotic suggestions can have tremendous power and benefits. Would you like to be able to give yourself a subconscious reminder to believe in yourself and pursue your dreams no matter what?

Allow me to give you a post-hypnotic suggestion to boost your success. This can take place consciously or unconsciously.

"Every time you see the number 2:22, you feel happiness and confidence germinating within you, like the seed of a mighty oak tree. The number 2:22 now represents a sign from your subconscious mind that you have what it takes to achieve your goals."

That suggestion will be as effective as you want it to be. The more frequently you act upon the following suggestion, repeating the phrase in your head every time you see 2:22, the more powerful it will become and the longer its effects will last.

I make sure to give my clients plenty of post-hypnotic suggestions that are relevant to them and their goals. Of course, these suggestions will be more powerful when they come from a Hypnotherapist. The thing that always amazes me is how my clients come back to their next session exclaiming, "It works! It works!"

Method # 15: How to Create a "Happiness Button"

Remember the story about the man that I hypnotized and now experiences a tremendous feeling of happiness whenever he makes a fist? I will teach you how to do the same thing, which will program your mind to trigger happiness. It is a Neuro-Linguistic Programming (NLP) technique called anchoring.

1. In a comfortable and safely-seated position, close your eyes and bring up a memory of feeling incredibly happy. Picture that memory in vivid detail. Take note of all of the positive things you are feeling.

2. Now make a fist. While thinking about that joyous memory, make a fist with your non-dominant hand. As you squeeze your fist, focus on spreading the happy feeling throughout your body, expanding it, making it as real as possible. Spend a few moments on this step.

3. Practice and repeat this method 10 times.

Once you have done so, stop squeezing your fist and open your eyes. Come back to the present moment. Now make a fist again with the same hand. Notice how you feel. Every time you squeeze your fist, your subconscious mind will be triggered to release a flood of happiness throughout your body. This is just like a muscle- the more you use it, the stronger it will become.

It is best to run through this exercise a few times in order to cement the suggestion into your subconscious mind so that the trigger becomes automatic and effective every time you use it, no matter where you are. This is one of the best secret weapons you will have, because nobody will even know what you are doing.

Once you have mastered this technique, you can start over with another feeling, such as confidence. For each different "button" you program, use a different physical trigger such as placing your hand over your heart, instead of making a fist, or holding onto a piece of jewelry, such as your wedding ring, while doing this technique.

The more often you repeat the new anchor, the more it becomes familiar to your mind and the closer you get to programming your mind to use this new pattern automatically.

To get the most out of this technique, allow me to walk you through it. I have created a video where you can experience it. Go to www.feelingpowerful.com/resources.

Instead of waiting to feel happy, calm or confident, program your mind to feel that way; give yourself reasons to feel the way you want to feel.

What action are you taking to love your life today?

What will you be doing to *live* your life today?

Chapter 17
The Art of Asking for What You Want

Featuring Mike Cantrell

> **Hypnotists' Secret # 11:**
> **The Power of Asking for What You Want**
>
> Hypnotists' entire shows rely on being able to ask people to do things, starting with asking volunteers to come up on stage.
> To successfully get what you want, you must know how to ask for what you want. This starts with pre-framing- which means to position yourself well. Be professional, confident, knowledgeable and have the right intentions. Clarify the outcome you want, and ask for it.
> *If you do not ask for what you want, the odds are that you will not get what you want.*

A major part of getting what you want comes from knowing how to ask for it.

There are many programs within the mind that cause you to think twice about expressing your desires. The most common ones are feeling unworthy of reaching your goals, fearing what others will think, fearing like you might look greedy, demanding or superficial, the fear of rejection, the fear of failure, and doubting yourself.

You can dramatically and positively influence all areas of your life by becoming proficient at making effective proposals.

Let's be clear- this is NOT expecting something for nothing or feeling entitled to getting things just because you asked for them.

This is about having the ability to know what you want, work for it, and speak to the right people about it in order to expedite the process, and make desirable things happen.

By having the ability to ask for what you want, you will be more effective in business, sales, leadership, relationships and your own personal fulfillment.

Whether you are asking God, the Universe, your subconscious mind or other people to help you attain your goals, there are some key elements in successfully creating and pitching what some people refer to as, "the big ask." There are ways to increase your odds of getting what you want- ethically, of course!

Whether or not you think you are in sales- you are. Every day you are pitching yourself to someone else. At the very least, you are attempting to sell people on your opinion.

You need to have the confidence and ability to ask for what you want because nobody is going to do it for you. Know what you want. Ask for it. Work for it.

**Hypnotists' Secret # 12:
The Power of Numbers**

Hypnotists understand that many of the volunteers who come onstage will be sent back to their seats leaving only a few participants on the stage. Instead of focussing on how many people are being sent back, the hypnotist concentrates on the remaining participants, knowing that they will be more than enough to provide entertainment.

No matter how good the hypnotist is, there will always be people who are told to return to their seats. Hypnotists know this and they work with it.

As with sales and most other things, it comes down to numbers. Some things will work out. Some things will not work out. Keep moving forwards anyway and avoid ruining the show because you are focused on the wrong thing.

What You Will and Will Not Get

It is important to note that you will not get everything you want in life.

And sometimes that can be the *best* thing that will ever happen to you because it opens you up to possibilities that are much greater and far beyond your conscious desires.

There will also be times where you get what you do *not* want in life.

This means there will be problems and situations that have a bad outcome despite your best efforts. Life is made up of experiencing love and loss, birth and death, sickness and health, acceptance and rejection, success and failure, light and dark, growth and decay.

Ask for what you want, anyways.

Go for it. Let yourself grow, improving upon what you want, and the way you go about it.

Life is Similar to Drilling for Oil

When a company is drilling for oil, there are times when they drill a hole, and the hole is dry- no oil in sight. Imagine everything that goes into drilling the hole, only to end up with nothing. While it is an ergonomic failure, Mike Cantrell, an oil and gas producer for 45 years, sees it as a geological success, because it reveals to you the areas that do not have the oil you are seeking, pointing you to the next location.

You will experience times where you come up short, or the outcome turns out to be the opposite of what you were expecting, despite doing everything within your power. The "dry holes" in life are there to nudge you in the right direction, if only you remain tenacious.

"Positive persistence for me was always drilling the next well or funding the next deal," states Mike, who has also helped high-ranking, well-known politicians to raise large sums of money for their campaigns, back when he was a Political Strategist. "My favorite word after experiencing failure is always, 'Next!'"

The Power of Positive Persistence

There may be days when you are not the only one doubting yourself and your abilities; others are, too.

"To be positively persistent first requires self-confidence," Mike observes. "I have always had confidence in myself even when others didn't. In fact, I have been motivated my entire life, to disprove nay-sayers. Others' lack of confidence in me propelled my own efforts."

In little league baseball, as a kid, Mike was overweight and never the first-chosen to be on any team. Rather than allowing that to bring him down, Mike would work harder to show them what he was made of, always making the all-star team, proving to everyone that hard work beats talent when those with talent do not work hard.

The long hours he dedicated to developing his skillsets at sports as a kid conditioned Mike's mind and work ethic for success later in his business.

Getting Out of the Dry Wells

"Success is going from failure to failure, without the loss of enthusiasm." Sir Winston Churchill.

"A positive attitude with the confidence in yourself to always move forward quickly will make failures feel like merely speed bumps in the road of life," Mike says. "While we should all learn lessons from our failures, dwelling on them just drags us down.

"Personally, I've known many failures. The principle I learned was to address every one of them by simply getting better. The best exercise for dealing with failure is to acknowledge it, understand it, then move forward with confidence and commitment to your goals."

You Are the Pilot, Your Life is the Plane

Have you ever set the goal of giving your entire life a makeover and felt the need to do it as quickly as possible, yet, after a few days of trying to create new habits and routines, you are back to where you started?

In his spare time, Mike learned how to become a pilot so that he could fly planes, achieving a long-time dream of his.

Flying an aircraft taught Mike a new perspective. "Learning to fly an airplane from one point to another is simply a matter of making small corrections. If you correct too much, you end up getting off course, sometimes to the point you get lost.

"Life is a lot like that. Most of us just need to make small corrections. When we over-correct we can get lost, or at least deferred from reaching our goals."

Creating a Successful Pitch

Before pitching your idea or opportunity to a potential business partner, sponsor, or financer, you must know what you want and why you want it.

According to Mike, who has succeeded in closing several lucrative business deals, including asking for and receiving significant sums of money, every pitch must contain these three key elements:

1. A Specific Purpose
2. A Specific Amount
3. By a Specific Time

Mike's 10 Crucial Steps to Asking Others for What You Want

1. Be there in Person

Eyeball to eyeball is the best way to raise money because people give significant amounts to *people*, not to letters, emails or phone calls.

2. Be a Friend

Donors need to feel friendship from those doing "the big ask." It is impossible to build friendships with all prospective donors, but you should do your best. Always treat the donor like a friend.

3. Be Persistent

Knowing your numbers will help you to be relentless. Mike goes by the rule of four; knowing that it takes him an average of four asks before he gets to the yes.

4. Model Your Donor

Get in sync with them and their communication style. People respond to those they feel are similar to themselves. If a donor likes to tell stories, listen. If the donor talks slow, then slow down your pace. If he or she talks quickly, speed up. If the donor is time conscious, make sure you are brief and to the point.

5. Be Sincere

You must believe in your cause. It is difficult to raise money for a plan, a purpose or a person you do not believe in. Most people can spot a phony a mile away. Pursue the causes you believe in.

6. Do Your Homework

Know your donor. Learn all you can about them, then pick one fact, subject or accomplishment of theirs which you can discuss with them. Anticipate questions. Know the answers.

7. Success Begets Success

It is always easier to raise specific amounts of money when others have done it.

8. Go Solo

It is usually more difficult to raise money if there is a group of people asking one donor. There can be a spoiler in a group setting, which means their negative attitude can dampen the attitudes and enthusiasm of others in the room. Make the donor feel important by giving them your undivided attention.

The exception: if you are among a small group of like-minded donors and you have at least one of them in on the deal already, this can set up social compliancy. This means that if one or more people in the group jump on the offer, others are more likely to, as well, due to the fact that the subconscious mind wants to remain compliant with the group. The other potential donors may think, "If she did it, I should do it, too!"

Use caution with this maneuver, as it can backfire. If the group is doubtful or opposed to the idea being pitched, this can cause the overall reaction of the group to turn the deal down, simply because everyone else is doing so.

9. Be Comfortable with the Silence

Once you ask for what you want, be confident and comfortable sitting in the silence. Remain silent and wait for the potential donor to be the first to speak. This is a crucial part of closing.

10. Follow Up
Be respectful of your donor's time and always, always, follow up. Even if the donor rejects your pitch, leave them with a good feeling about the visit.

And follow up!

Leadership = Power

"Power corrupts," Mike says, "unless it is tempered by love and responsibility. Obtaining any kind of power requires working with others. In other words, it requires leadership.

"Maintaining power requires using it responsibly and with love and care for others. Power that lasts is not only shared but is distributed to others. The highest form of leadership is leading others to be leaders.

"The highest exercise of power would reach its pinnacle when it is given away."

Being Happy with or without what You Want

Mike is one of the happiest people you will ever meet. He is one of those rare persons who loves the life he has and enjoys where he is, while greeting each day with enthusiasm and a positive outlook.

"True happiness doesn't come from things or even people," Mike says. "True happiness comes from some form of inner spiritual strength that starts with the faith that life is unfolding as it should.

"Happiness isn't created, it is accepted. It begins with awareness and ends with gratefulness."

Mike Cantrell has been an oil and gas producer for 45 years. He is also a political strategist, issue activist, author, and association builder.

He and his wife Linda live in Ada, Oklahoma with their two adult children and four grandchildren.

For more information visit www.MikeCantrell.net

Chapter 18
Own Your Power

Stop Giving Away Your Power!

If you are serious about feeling your absolute best and becoming your most powerful self, you must stop giving away your power.

The most common ways you make yourself powerless are by complaining, having victim mentality, dwelling on negativity, gossiping, judging others, and blaming others.

We all have flaws and times of weakness. Be kind and forgiving to everyone, including yourself.

More Ways to Optimize Your Mind and Maximize Your Power

While your mind is extremely powerful, it is important to use a well-rounded approach to help yourself get from point A to point B. Remember, your mind and body are both affected by each other, so, take care of both.

Your thoughts affect your actions and your actions affect your thoughts. Below is a list of a few actions that can help you to create a happy, healthy and balanced mind.

Remember, you are your habits.

Your habits happen on autopilot without much conscious thought or effort- if any at all.

When you change your habits, you change your life.

Eat Healthier

The food you eat influences the way your mind functions and the way you feel. Personally, I have found that when I eat sugar and processed foods it makes it more difficult for me to think positively and feel happy. When I eat healthier foods, I feel

Power Now

like I have better control over my mind and emotions. Find a nutritionist to work with you and discover which foods help boost your mood. It makes a dramatic difference.

Exercise

Everybody knows exercise is important to keep the body strong and healthy. Exercise is also necessary in order to help the mind function at its best.

Do you ever notice how stagnant ponds are full of scum and look disgusting while water in a waterfall or flowing in a river is clean and clear? If the human body is made up of a large majority of water, doesn't it make sense to get the body moving?

The mind is the same way- it is clearest when it is moving. I notice a huge difference in my mindset, creativity and mood when I exercise at least a few times per week. When I get "into the zone," ideas seem to "download" into my mind.

Make sure you are exercising the correct way in order to maximize your results. Hire a trainer, even just to get started. Find someone who motivates you. Personally, I am a big fan of the personal trainer, Darin Steen. Named the Next Great Trainer by Arnold Schwarzenegger, Darin has a wonderful motivational attitude, has trained the well-known Dr. Mercola, and he is as big as WWE's John Cena. He has online transformational programs available at www.fatlosslifestyle.com.

Get Out in Nature

Go for a hike in the forest. Walk along the beach. Sit in the park. This is my favorite therapy. Within minutes of being in a forest, I automatically feel happier and calmer. It's like an all-natural "high."

Practice Mindfulness

This is a technique of using your awareness to focus on the present. When you do this properly, it is a form of meditation without having to sit still.

It can be as simple as taking three deep breaths and using your awareness to follow your breaths as you inhale and exhale. When you do this, it automatically brings you into the present moment. Focus on one thing only- your current task at hand. If you are talking to a loved one, focus on hearing what they are saying, instead of listening to the voice in your head and how you intend to respond.

You will know you are living in the present when you have reached acceptance of what is, when you are beginning to feel calmer, more grounded, centred, peaceful, happy and powerful.

The mind tends to drift back to the past or forward to the future, so be patient with yourself and practice mindfulness throughout the day.

Do a Social Media Cleanse

Do you find yourself starting to become overwhelmed by negativity or the obsession of comparing your life to the lives of others online? Do a social media cleanse. Social media is meant to be a tool to help you spread your message, but, it sometimes has a negative impact on the mind. If you find that it leaves you feeling drained, you may want to assess how you are using this tool.

Follow the accounts that motivate and inspire you and unfollow the ones that trigger negative effects. Change the way you view the platform: social media is not meant to cause you to compare yourself to others who have a "better life" than you. It is intended to help you connect with those who are like-minded. Prevent overwhelm by scheduling posts or hiring someone to help you and know when you need to take a breather from it.

Write Your Goals Down

"Power is freedom." Rachel David.

Rachel David seemingly had it all: a job on TV with a clothing allowance, while also travelling the world and dating a wrestler in WWE. Then she got laid off from her job and her boyfriend broke up with her at the same time. The hardest thing about that time for Rachel was that she did not know who she was. She turned to YouTube and posted a video about her troubling situation and told the world this video would keep her accountable as she worked hard to get through this time and come out on top.

During that time, a couple of friends told her, "Rachel, you have to write down your goals and email it to a few friends. It works." She listed ten things, including details such as: when she wants to have kids, when she wants to be in a relationship, where her boyfriend will be living, how much money she wants to make, the body size she wants to be and what she wants to be known for.

Rachel says, "Out of the ten things, over half of them have been completed faster. It comes back to accountability. Set a really big goal that you almost can't achieve. It will keep you going." From the depths of despair, Rachel took action and eventually became an influential YouTuber and the owner of her own company.

In fact, after my discussion with Rachel, I had a look at my own dreams and goals and I rewrote them in greater detail. And most of those dreams came true so quickly, I could barely believe it.

Write down big goals. Stop playing small.

Love Yourself

How many times do your eyes automatically go to the areas of your body you dislike each time you look in the mirror? This trains your mind to focus on those areas and will consequently diminish your self-confidence.

First thing in the morning, in a mirror, look yourself in the eye and say out loud, "I love you," and find three things you like about yourself. This is conditioning your mind to love yourself and find the positive. It can transform your self-confidence and self-love within days!

Empower Others

If a beautiful woman walks into the room and you find yourself mentally picking her apart, finding her flaws, seeing her as competition and listing reasons why you dislike her, you have low self-confidence. A confident person is one who can look at another confident and successful person and feel happy for their success.

If you find yourself feeling a lack of confidence or jealousy around other powerful people, catch those negative thoughts right away and mentally list three things you like about that person and wish them further success.

Weak people tear others down and strong people build others up. Decide which type of person you want to be and act accordingly.

Create Balance

When you create balance in your life it will help you to create balance in your mind and vice versa. Practice moderation and self-discipline. Just because you can do whatever you want does not mean that you should. Practicing discipline and moderation daily will help create a mind that is stronger and healthier.

Get Help

Some of the best decisions I have ever made and the times when I have accelerated the most are when I hired a coach. I got over my pride, admitted I needed help and hired an expert to push me outside of my comfort zone and reach new levels. The insight, the strategies and the accountability were worth their weight in gold.

Ever notice how the most successful people, such as athletes, always have coaches, while the least successful people only get the opinions of those closest to them?

The best investment is in yourself.

Get into a Flotation Tank

Also known as a sensory deprivation tank, a flotation tank is filled with body temperature salt water that is so buoyant you feel as if there is no gravity. There are no lights or sounds, which means you give your mind and body a deeply peaceful and restorative break from constantly being stimulated. Floating helps you to find your knowledge within, which empowers you through your current situation.

Just as minimalism is a growing trend for people to escape the pressures of society and find their peace by cutting down on the excess clutter in their life, float tanks are like minimalism for your body and mind. A lot of people are turning to flotation therapy as a means of dealing with emotional and physical pain and they are attaining significant results.

Tips for getting the most out of your float: Once the tank's lights have turned off, I recommend thinking of something that makes you incredibly happy. This can be a past memory, a hobby you are passionate about, a loved one, or something you look forward to. Really focus on that good feeling and intensify it.

Then become the observer of your mind and watch the adventure it will take you on from there!

During your float session, use self-hypnosis and ask your mind what area of yourself you need to work on, heal or improve. Then surrender to the silence and allow your mind to bring the answers to you. Gently ask your mind for solutions.

Essential Oils

Something that I love to use to help me unwind, destress or boost my mood are essential oils in a diffuser. As for which essential oil to use, that all depends upon the fragrance you prefer and your goal. Some oils are stimulating and others are relaxing.

Instant Mood Boost

I diffuse a couple drops of tangerine oil or peppermint oil in the A.M. It perks up my mood, clears my mind, and helps me to feel happy, even on a dark day.

Instant Relaxer

To help me unwind, relax and sleep better in the P.M., I diffuse a couple drops of lavender oil or chamomile oil, starting it about an hour before I go to sleep.

EFT (Emotional Freedom Technique)

This is otherwise known as tapping and is an acupressure technique using your fingertips to gently tap different areas of the body to help promote emotional health, which can in turn affect physical health. It is often paired with a form of a mantra.

This technique can be used as a means of dealing with mental and emotional blockages. It can be a great way to deal with emotions and release negativity.

There are several instructional videos available for free online. Find an instructor who resonates with you.

Program Your Mind with Hypnosis

Hypnotherapy is growing in popularity and people are turning to it to help them fully utilize the power of their subconscious minds and reach their goals.

Find out what it feels like to be hypnotized in the comfort of your own home! Go to my website and I will send you access to one of my most popular hypnosis recordings for FREE! See you at www.feelingpowerful.com/resources.

Join the Feeling Powerful Community

Do you get overwhelmed at the thought of doing it all yourself? Do you want more clarity, focus and peace of mind knowing that you are on the right path?

Imagine being able to start your day off in such a powerful way, that you feel in control throughout the events of the day. Imagine what it would feel like to be able to control how each day begins, so that you can build momentum throughout the day and feel extremely proud of yourself by the time your head hits the pillow that night.

Program your mind to be its best every day and notice how your life starts to transform. You can program your mind to feel happier, more confident, satisfied, brave and fulfilled. Go to www.feelingpowerful.com/go to get started now. Your best life is waiting.

Bonus Chapter
Experts' Success Stories

"*On Monday, Wednesday, Friday I think I'm pretty great. On Tuesday, Thursday, Saturday I think I'm the biggest failure. On Sunday I don't even know what to think. Can you relate?*" [4] David Foster: Canadian Musician, Record Producer, Composer, Songwriter, and Arranger.

Some of the best opportunities for redesigning your subconscious mind will present themselves through the various obstacles, opposition and pain you face. You can accelerate the process by learning from others who have accomplished admirable feats. Several aspirational experts from various industries allowed me intimate access to their minds so that I can share their powerful words of wisdom with you in these pages.

The laws of the subconscious mind remain the same- despite your goals or current set of circumstances. There are many methods for getting what you want; however, the most value you will discover in your life comes from the ability to change your mind.

Triumphing and Creating Success

W. Brett Wilson: Season Three Panelist on CBC TV's Dragon's Den, Investment Banker, Businessman, Entrepreneur, Philanthropist, Author, Two-Time Cancer Survivor. You see people from all walks of life going on shows like Dragon's Den, seeking money, partnerships, knowledge and guidance from the wise experts sitting before them- the investors. One of the former Dragons, W. Brett Wilson, revealed to me some crucial mind-altering concepts.

Power Now

"First, you must challenge the definition of success."

"The typical definition of success is a relatively shallow and superficial measure of wealth. In a wealth-obsessed world, we're all looking at how big is the other's house, how expensive is  their car, where they spend their vacations, and what they wear. Sometimes this whole gamut of chasing success without defining it first- and properly- is a recipe for a large wallet and a failed life."

What about a man who has achieved some of the highest levels of success, according to society's standards- has he failed?

Yes.

Nearly every person that I interviewed for this book told me their most instructive lesson came from trusting the wrong people.

Brett explains, "There have been failures in terms of choosing partners. Good people can figure out how to make apple sauce out of fallen apples. Bad people can take a great business and destroy it quickly."

How did this sharp-minded man flip his mindset and continue on towards achieving his big goals?

"I've come to accept that failure is not terminal, it is a stepping stone to another level. Failure doesn't shut down a concept, a product or a business. It just means you have to redirect.

"When it comes to failure, think about it as driving a car: you cannot drive by only staring in the rear-view mirror. You have to look out the windshield. Basically, when people dwell on

Power Now

failure, they're living in the past as opposed to allowing themselves to move forwards.

"We pay way too much attention to people's mistakes. I acknowledge that I'm still making mistakes with family relationships and some of the businesses that I invest in. I don't beat myself up about it- I simply move on."

How Brett Conquers his Mindset

How do you press forward when things did not go as planned? You need to be in control of your mindset, switching it to focus on the outcome you want.

Business-savvy Brett shares the uplifting affirmation that has become the traditional axiom in the world of sales: "The next call will be the sale." This invaluable affirmation plants seeds of hope into the subconscious.

"The most important thing," Brett concludes, "whether you're trying to get your day going or you're trying to get your business going, you need an element of discipline. If people can't get focussed, their outcomes are haphazard."

Creating a Life Full of Accomplishments and Happiness

Graham Lee: President and CEO of GSL Group, one of Canada's leading commercial/recreational development and operations companies, owner of the WHL team, Victoria Royals.

Graham Lee is deemed successful by all of society's standards. Even more inspirational than his accomplishments are the noticeable feelings of inner peace and true happiness that radiate from him.

Although, it should be known, things were not always that way for him.

Around age five, Graham would often visit his neighbour's yard and he would notice that they had better toys than him. The neighbour's playthings were newer and shinier. His were old and beat-up.

He remembers returning home one day and thinking, "Why would I want that other toy car if I can't have it? I might as well want what I have and think of it as the best there is. Even though my toy's beaten up, I'm happy with it."

Graham went on to say, "I didn't want what the other kid had anymore, because I found my happiness with what I had." This created his sense of contentment and became a major lesson that has stuck with him ever since.

"I learned to want what I have instead of have what I want."

"I conditioned my mind at a very young age- it wasn't about business back then. It was about the toys."

When Graham was starting his business, he had this underlying confidence in himself that he knew he could achieve whatever he wanted. Graham remembers, "Before I went to bed every night, I'd say to myself, 'You can do it,' reinforcing my outlook on things and giving myself more confidence, even though I was already fairly self-assured."

Today, Graham continues to visualize his goals and see the bigger picture. "When it comes to business, I envision specific goals. I picture our company and the people around us and the change in environment, the reactions of people and seeing them once we have accomplished that. I put myself into that picture."

How Graham Lives to his Highest Potential

"You have to know where you don't want to be. If you don't want to be living the life that you have right now, or you don't think it's the right opportunity for you, you're not living to your highest potential.

"You have to overcome those fears of failure, fears of not succeeding and keep that end goal in mind. Failure is just lessons along the way. You must learn from them and say, 'How do I avoid it again?'

The $25,000 Lesson

"When I was in my twenties, I got into a business and it turned out the partner was dishonest. I ended up losing $25,000, which was a lot of money back then. I've been through a lot of these challenges along the way, but again, every challenge was a lesson."

Graham continues to condition his mind for what he wants, "Mental preparation is required," he advises, "in order to achieve your highest potential. Whether it is developing a routine or getting rid of that conditioned negative voice in your head, whatever it is, you need to focus on doing the best you can every day. You've got to master your own mind. You can't be a passenger.

"Power is when you have the luxury of time to do whatever you want to do to achieve your goals. Once you get past that stage of the short-term income and you start doing things much bigger than yourself, that's when you can feel you've really succeeded."

Power Now

Conquering Yourself... And the Competition!
Vadim Garbuzov: Five-Time World Champion in Show Dance, Three-Time European Show Dance Champion, Two-Time Winner of Austrian Dancing with the Stars- and Canadian Youth Champion in all disciplines.

When Vadim first started dreaming of becoming a professional dancer, several people tried to discourage him, telling him his goal would be impossible to attain. The odds of becoming a professional dancer for a living are very slim, and there is a lot of competition.

What happens when the world tells you your dreams are too big or too difficult to attain?

In Vadim's case, the discouragement became a driving force, pushing him to want his goals even more. He felt like he owed it to them to make it happen, because they had given up on their own dreams somewhere along the line. Vadim wanted to inspire his friends and family with his own success, asserting,

"Deep down, I held onto the belief that I *could* achieve my goals."

How Vadim Programmed his Mind like a Champion

As you can imagine, there are many twists and turns along the path of becoming a world-class dancer. Along his trajectory of winning competitions and trophies, Vadim learned how to conquer himself. He would get up early every single day to train-whether he felt like it or not.

"There were many times when I wanted to give up. During those times I would visualize my goals with specific details, including how it would feel to win and picturing myself holding the exact trophy I wanted. There was a constant conviction in my subconscious mind that I had to win… and that I *could* win. I knew it deep down."

Inside the Mind of a Winner

Besides the long hours of practicing and routines, Vadim worked on his mind. "Every single day I would spend time visualizing myself achieving my goals and creating the feeling of having already achieved my desires. I even had posters of the trophies on my walls. I surrounded myself with my goals."

When it comes to obtaining the number one spot in show dance competitions, you could say Vadim has winning down to a science. He seems to hit every target he sets his eyes upon. How does this top-notch, prize-winning dancer access and direct the power of his mind towards achieving his desires?

Vadim's Top 5 Tips for Reaching Your Goals

1. Visualize

It's important. See what you want and hold it in your mind

2. Stay Persistent

If it is something you really desire, keep moving forward and stay persistent. Work on your goals daily, *even when you don't feel like it.*

3. Keep a Positive Mindset

Read books about self-improvement and the power of the mind.

4. Continue to Challenge Yourself

Challenges help you learn and grow.
5. Get a Good Coach.
"It makes a difference. I am grateful for the supportive coaches I have had along my journey. They have been a big help."

After achieving his lifelong dream, Vadim was at a loss for what to do next.

So, he fixed his mind on another goal. Vadim is now working towards his current ambition of setting a world record by becoming the first seven-time winner of the World Champion title in show dance…

And perhaps he will go on to becoming the first eight-time winner, after that.

You can cheer him on and follow his story at www.vadimgarbuzov.com.

Replacing Victim Mindset with Victory Mindset

Jennie Diaz: wife and partner of Alex Ricardo Diaz; a Senior Vice President at Primerica. They went from being financially broke and mentally devastated, to becoming financially free, while leading others to do the same.

We often blame our parents for the problems in our lives today. We hold onto this blame, resentment and anger and sooner or later it bleeds into several areas of our lives. The negative experiences from the past have programmed us and shaped us into who we are today. And all of that can change, if you are willing to reprogram your subconscious mind.

Jennie Diaz grew up with parents who were members of a gang. They were not around much while she was young and she never got to hear them say, "I love you." She felt like a victim. When she became an adult, she realized, "If I don't change that mentality, I'm still a victim."

While starting out in her current line of business, Jennie became aware of how much victim mentality had a negative impact on her life. You give away all of your power when you blame other people. While it is not your fault for what happened in your childhood, it is your responsibility as an adult to move forward. You gain your power back by taking responsibility for creating what you want.

How Jennie Overcame Victim Mentality

"I started seeking out others who were happy, and they would tell me which books they read. I read those books. I didn't think about changing others around me- the only person I thought about changing was myself. Every day I would get better and work on myself. Eventually, everybody around me became better, because I chose to have better people around me.

"If you're at the point in your life where you're so tired of where you're at, where every breath you take is bad, then you're ready for change. You have to be the one to seek your change. The minute that happens, your life changes forever. My advice for anybody is change yourself. By changing yourself, your life around you changes."

How Jennie Rewired her Mind for Victory

1. Morning Intentions. "The first thing I do in the morning is thank God. I say a little prayer, 'Today is the day that You woke me up. What are we going to accomplish together? Today I'm going to be the best that I can be in my life.' The first 5 things you tell yourself in the morning really determine what your day's going to look like."

2. Daily Reflections. "Ask yourself every single night, 'What did I learn today that can make me better?' People often say, 'I've had a bad day.' It wasn't a bad day, it was a bad minute or a bad five minutes. You determine how long you're going to allow that bad time to last- it doesn't determine you."

3. Affirmation and Visualization Wall. "I have an affirmation wall and an accomplishment wall. I do a dream board with my daughter every three months. In three months, your life can really change if you just make the decision and put your head down to get to where you want to go."

"Power: the minute you stop caring about other people's opinions, you have power over your life. When you start thinking about how others feel about you, you're just giving your power away."

Creating a Mindset for Success

Denise Flores: wife and partner of Martin Romulo Flores; a Vice President at Primerica. They spent decades investing in improving their mindsets and finances while teaching and leading other people to do so for themselves.

When you see a successful person, do you ever find yourself wondering if they have days, or even moments, of lacking self-confidence?

Denise admits, "Almost every day, there are times where I don't believe in myself."

It is reassuring to know that others feel what we feel, even if they are walking a different path than we are. Denise has discovered the key to refocusing the power of her subconscious towards designing the life she wants. "I remind myself of what my goals are. The main thing is to remind myself that I want to be something more than average. I've always strived to be the best that I can be."

The Rejection Projection Complex

Many people take rejection personally, which will have an obvious detrimental effect if you are in the world of sales. All too often, when we face opposition to our idea or sales pitch, we allow the stories in our minds to take over and spiral downwards. We project our insecurities onto others and then feel we are being turned down because of our flaws.

As someone who does a lot of cold prospecting in her career, Denise reveals that she used to have inferiority complexes so strong, it was difficult to get out of bed some mornings. She overcame these mental challenges by reading personal development books. "The more I read the more I realized, when you face rejection, people aren't rejecting you-they're rejecting whatever you're offering them. People will reject you because either the information you gave them wasn't clear and they didn't understand what you were offering, or they don't believe in themselves."

As a kid, Denise was teased and bullied. She later came to realize, "It wasn't that I was the one with the issues- they were taking their issues out on me." This early life experience taught Denise valuable lessons that she now profits from in business.

Surround Yourself with Your Dreams and Your Dreams will become Your Surroundings

Several successful people are known for using dream boards: placing images of the lifestyle they want in front of them and having it as a constant subliminal reminder. Denise walks the walk. "I have a dream board in my office," she says. "We're constantly talking about our dreams. Many of them have come true: new cars, our business, our income. If I don't have a goal and focus on it, it's not going to happen."

Imagine that you invested a bit of time and effort each day into programming your mind to achieve your ambitions on autopilot. That is exactly what Denise has accomplished. "Now, it's like second nature. If we want something- it's a mindset," she says.

How powerful is that- what you want is a *mindset*.

"Don't think about the how- think about how you want it to end. Power is having the ability to change people's lives for the better."

Developing Wealth through Personal Development

Hector LaMarque: a top Senior National Sales Director at Primerica. He went from earning $50,000 per year working in a jewelry store to making a few million dollars per year in passive income, building an empire of 12,000 agents.

How does it sound to live every day as if you are on vacation?

That is the reality for Hector LaMarque and his wife after building a lucrative company worth millions of dollars in the financial industry.

Growing up in a small house with nine people and no money, Hector did not encounter a successful person until he was a young adult. He realized that he wanted to live every day on his own terms, and that in order to do so, he would need to build a substantial stream of passive income. He worked hard to make that happen.

How Hector Created a Mindset of Prosperity

1. Master Rejection and Sales. Rejection lets you see behind the curtain of your character, revealing your fears, insecurities and weaknesses. While that becomes too much for some people and they reach a breaking point, others choose to see rejection as a lesson and work on developing themselves by changing their mindsets.

Hector elaborates, "The problem is very few people ever do the necessary work to grow their skillsets to the point where they can be successful. They think the people who succeed are lucky; they don't see the work that successful people put into being successful.

"Nobody likes rejection. The better your skillsets are, the less rejection you'll have. I didn't like rejection at all. I knew that if I improved my skills, I could minimize the amount of rejection, and that's exactly what happened."

2. Write Your Goals Down. "I write down what I want to accomplish. I have a summary of it, because there are a lot of things. I put it everywhere- the mirror in my bathroom, on my

fridge, my bedroom, the sun visor or my car, my cellphone. I'm seeing my goals all the time. I'm thinking about them all the time.

"What we think about relentlessly overtime, we create in our physical reality. Most people don't focus to the extent that they need to. Your subconscious mind helps you to create it."

3. Focus on What You Want. "People struggle with it because it doesn't happen overnight. It may take years. If you keep working towards it, you can make it happen. It doesn't have anything to do with education; it has to do with mindset.

"People may not realize they're using the power of focus, but that's what it is. Do it on purpose. Most people don't think about it. It is lack of awareness. Everybody does it. If they want a new car, they see the car they want everywhere they go and they picture it all the time, talking about it non-stop. They're thinking about it relentlessly and they find a way to make it happen.

"You have to learn how to do it on purpose. Most people never learn that, which is why they struggle."

4. Be Relentless. "The main thing I discovered is that everybody who has achieved something great has encountered obstacles along the way.

"The difference between people who succeed and the ones who don't succeed, is the successful ones keep going, regardless of what is in front of them. They just don't let up. Eventually, they break through to the other side. Most people give up when they have daunting challenges."

5. Take Action. "It's not just about thinking, it's about acting on the thinking. Thinking is critical because thinking creates your actions, and your actions create your results. To start with, it's really about how you think, but then you have to act and do the work. Most people don't do it.

"They think it is something outside of them that is causing them to struggle, when it is really something within themselves that is causing the struggle."

6. Manage Yourself. "Reading books or listening to audio programs is important. Even if you don't know what to do,

somebody has already done it and knows what to do. I've probably read over 1500 books about personal development. I've been to countless seminars and have probably spent over $150,000 on personal development over the last 35 years or so.

"There are no short cuts. That's what you must do. It's about managing yourself and getting yourself to do the work.

"If I can do it, anybody can do it. It's really your thinking and actions, of course. The ones who are successful are the ones who are committed to personal development. It's not that complicated. It's very simple. It takes work.

"Power is the ability to manage the way you think and act. It is really all about self-management."

Achieving Your Dreams-Your Way

Nigel Bullers: CEO of EasyPark, an innovative parking company paving the way for sustainability and winning several awards; former Vice President of Famous Players.

Besides achieving your desires, one of the most satisfying "wins" is knowing that you did it your way, and that you remained authentic to yourself.

Nigel Bullers is a man who has done just that. Through hard work and a mind full of unconventional ideas and without formal college education, Nigel worked hard and earned himself the position of the CEO of EasyPark.

This CEO, known for thinking outside the box, says it's a good thing when your ideas do not work out.

You read that correctly.

Nigel explains, "It's not the ideas that work that you have to find because they're really hard- that's like looking for a needle in a haystack. What you have got to do is find the hay and sweep it aside while looking for the needle. If you just start getting rid of the hay, what's left? The needle.

"Dealing with obstacles is a way of discovering something really unique, a kind of treasure you would never have found. For me, it's really about what you discover in the process of ripping away an obstacle. If you're reading this and you're still asking yourself, 'Why did I fail?' The answer is, you haven't failed, you just haven't succeeded the way you want to yet."

How Nigel Turned his Vision into a Reality

Nigel explains: "If you think about the really great business leaders in the world, such as Walt Disney or Conrad Hilton, they all started with a story in their head, which they would call a vision. The things that they were building didn't exist; they were just in their head. If you envision yourself and picture yourself someplace different and you keep at that over and over, you will eventually get there."

What do you do during those times where your dreams are so big and there is no apparent way of getting there?

Nigel emphasizes that it is not important to know *how* you will achieve your goal. The importance lies in holding onto that goal and moving towards it. "If you dream that big," Nigel explains, "the appearance of those options will show up and you will become open to seeing them when they come. Take a leap of faith in yourself and life."

"You've got to start with a vision." Which is exactly what Nigel did. If Nigel were to look back at the goals he set as a fifteen-year-old, including the car he wanted, the lifestyle he fantasized about, and the exotic places he wanted to visit, he has arrived at exactly where he dreamed he would be. At that time, he told everyone his vision and the others would say to him, "Well, how are you ever going to be able to do all that?" And he remembers saying to them, "I don't know; I'm just going to do it."

And he did.

"Power is the ability to control your own life and your choices. Real power is making the choice to change."

Committing to Yourself No Matter What

Jan Bell Irving: Former President of Junior Achievement of BC; and an Inspirational Warrior, surviving four different types of cancer.

There may be times where you lose all faith in yourself and you turn to someone else in the hopes of being uplifted. Be mindful of whom you give that power to, making sure they are in your corner.

At the age of 29, Jan was diagnosed with cancer for the first time. "I was completely freaked out," she said. "I was sure I was going to die."

Jan's outlook was changed forever during a conversation with her doctor when she asked him what her odds of survival were. The doctor looked at her and said, "You know Jan, why would I ever tell you what your odds are? Your odds are 100%. Even if you had a 1 percent chance of survival, why would you not believe you would be that 1%?"

"And I have believed in that 1% ever since," Jan proudly states.

How Jan Continues to Win Every Battle

When it comes to triumphing through the toughest of times, Jan seems to have a secret to her success. "Frankly there is no alternative to absolute commitment to yourself and absolute belief in yourself.

"Just because you believe in yourself does not necessarily mean things are going to go your way. I think it's just the starting point and I think you really need to try and be organized and you need to ask for what you want." Self-determination is crucial.

"Power: it's not getting it your own way all the time. It is having faith in others and letting go of the need for control."

Finding Your Purpose through Finding Yourself

Connor Beaten: founder and CEO of Man Talks, empowerment seminars for men's health, wellness, success and fulfillment. He has delivered a speech on the stage of Tedx Vancouver, BC, Canada.

You may find it hard to believe that Connor Beaton, now the leader of international empowerment seminars for men, once had a negative fixed mindset stuck on the things he was unable to achieve.

At rock bottom, Connor was living out of his car and about to lose a couple hundred thousand dollars in a business deal that had gone sour. On the brink of declaring bankruptcy, he decided he could not take one more moment of being negative.

He made the choice to believe that he could overcome anything placed in his way and he created a mantra, writing it down on a sticky note and posting it where he would see it every day. It read, "I can overcome any obstacle and I can face any fear."

Although that sticky note may be a little tattered now, it is in the exact place he stuck it years ago and he claims it helped him to get through the harsh times. Having found his purpose, Connor is now on a mission to help others to find theirs as well.

What is your mantra? Create one for yourself.

How Connor Found Purpose

"Purpose is a spaceship and passion is the fuel. Passion will *fuel* your purpose, but it is not necessarily your purpose. Your purpose in life will always be so much bigger than you.

"Our purpose is not about us specifically. It is about what we can do for other people. Passion is about us, purpose is about others. Steven Covey says, 'Begin with the end in mind.' That is so applicable to life- how we want to go out."

"Power: most people are familiar with the saying, 'With great power comes great responsibility.' I believe it is the other way around: with great responsibility comes great power."

From Three Jobs to Dream Job

Desmond Liew: Director, International Development & Operations, Bing Han Ginseng. He went from envying the luxurious lives of others to creating the life of his dreams, while at the same time helping others.

At one point Desmond was working two full time jobs and one part-time job- all at the same time.

While helping a wealthy business owner pick up a few items she had purchased at an expensive retail store, Desmond's perspective unexpectedly expanded. He became inspired by the freedom and the lifestyle she had. From that day forward, Desmond committed himself to working hard to accomplish the same lifestyle for himself, planting the idea of his success deeply into his mind, knowing that it was possible.

He now works his dream job, travelling the world and leading a health food company through international expansion. He says that learning about how money works and making proper decisions gave him the right fuel to reach his goals.

"Your mind is so powerful. Just focus on what you want, tell your mind you want it, and then *be* that person."

How Desmond became a Leader

While you *can* succeed on your own, Desmond shares that having the right team of people in place will help you to accelerate along the path of reaching your desires.

Now, more than ever, people are "following" others, creating platforms and opportunities for new leaders to step up.

There is a difference between being a leader with a following and being a leader who can influence their following.

A motivational leader can nudge people towards a path that can change their lives for the better. Desmond would know, as he does this throughout the world, inspiring others to create the life they want. He says, "As a leader, instead of telling people you want them to believe in you, you have to *become* the person they can believe in."

"Power is the ability to give. You're most powerful when you can give and not ask for anything in return."

Conclusion

Your Success

Wait- There's More!

When it comes to the mind, it can be easy to overlook how far you have come unless you stop and consciously consider it.

Now it is time to look at where you are, by answering the following questions:

1. Document where you are now. Be honest with yourself:

a.) On a scale of 1-10, where are you in terms of reaching your goals? (1= far away from your goals, 10= you have already reached them.)

b.) On a scale of 1-10, how do you feel about the life you are living? (1= unhappy, 10= you are living your best life.)

c.) How do you generally feel about yourself? List any emotions or thought patterns that you frequently experience.

d.) On a scale of 1-10, how do you feel about your ability to control your mind? (1= you have no control, 10= you can control it well.)

e.) How much time do you spend taking care of your mind each day? Include meditation, visualization, therapy, reading, etc.

f.) Document the details of where you are now. Take a picture of yourself; take note of your stress level, your job situation, your relationship satisfaction and anything else that is important to you. It is necessary to know these things in order to evaluate your success.

g.) In what areas of your mind (or your life) do you notice improvements? (More self-control, ability to change your mindset, increased positive thinking, etc.)

h.) What goals have you achieved recently? (Do you notice more happiness, inner peace, confidence, etc.?)

i.) Reassess your goals: which ones are you on target to achieve? Which ones need some adjustment? What goals would you like to add to the list?

j.) Stop where You Are and Review the Journey

Remember those questions you answered at the beginning of this book? It is time to compare your first answers with where you are now and feel proud about your journey. You may have heard it said before, "It is not about the destination, it is about the journey."

As much as we all love to get to our desired destinations safely and in a timely manner, occasionally we have to take a pause, and look at how far we have come. That is something worth being proud of. Make sure to do this every so often- because it will benefit your mind.

Keep your answers in a safe and handy place where you will remember where they are. Create a habit of self-assessing every 2-4 weeks so that you can see which areas are improving and which ones need some tweaking.

Everything taught to you in this book is meant to give you strategies to reprogram your mind and live your best life. These skills are meant to be practiced on a regular basis throughout your life. They will get easier with time, and one day they will be a natural way of being. Reread this book and apply the methods often, to keep yourself on track.

Before you know it, you will be able to program your mind to achieve just about anything.

Suggestions for Your Success

Here is a list of suggestions I "suggest" that you use to help reprogram your mind. Feel free to make them your own.

- "I belong here."
- "Today is going to be a fantastic day."
- "Today is the day. Now is the time. I choose to create change now."
- "I commit to my success."

- "I give myself permission to be my best self now."
- "I choose to experience more peace and joy today."
- "It is becoming easier for me to create positive change."
- "I am becoming better every day."
- "I let go of the things that no longer benefit me and choose to focus on what brings me joy."
- "My mind will guide me in the right direction,"
- "This is leading me to something better."
- "I always win: either I learn a lesson or a blessing."
- "Challenges give me the opportunity to become a better version of myself and they nudge me in the right direction when I take inspired action."
- "Something wonderful is about to happen."
- "My true self is free. I am free to be me."
- "I attract the best people and opportunities into my life."
- "I choose to fill my day with purpose, love, happiness and fulfillment."
- "I value myself, my feelings and my health."
- "I am worthy of all of the greatness that life has to offer."
- "I am a blessing unto others."
- "Today I am doing something that will satisfy my soul."
- "I surrender. The solutions will come."
- "This is only a phase and it will lead me to something better, as long as I am persistent and open minded. When I get through it, I will be that much better because of it. I am grateful for this journey."
- "I forgive you. I love you. Thank you."

Work with Me!
It's Time to become Your Most Powerful Self!

Do you feel overwhelmed, stuck, or alone on this journey?

Are you curious about what your life could look like if you were to tap into your inner potential and become your best self?

You can receive my guidance and support to accelerate the process. Let's work together. I have a virtual office, which means you can have my guidance and support from the comfort of your own home.

"Working with Kirsten was one of the best experiences of my life... I think everyone should experience hypnotherapy with Kirsten." Bianca, Vancouver

The Most Common Reasons People Come to Work with Me:

1. They feel a bit stuck and lost and like there is a part of them they need to fix. They know that with the right guidance, they can create a life they love.

2. They are on top of their game, always seeking ways to grow and transform. They want to give themselves an edge; making the most out of themselves and getting the most out of life.

3. They want to broaden their horizons, expand their minds and explore all that life has to offer. They are on a spiritual journey and seek inner peace, balance and fulfilling the desires of their soul.

My Methods are Fantastic for:
- Destressing in the Workplace
- Increasing Productivity
- Boosting Confidence, Self-Worth and Self-Love
- Changing Your Mindset
- Increasing Motivation
- Decreasing Fear and Strengthening Courage
- Gaining Skills to Cope with the Highs and Lows of Life
- Boosting Happiness
- Getting in Tune with Yourself
- Relaxing, Refreshing, and Renewing Your Mind
- Fulfilling Your Dreams
- Creating a Satisfying Life
- Optimizing Your Potential and becoming the Best Version of Yourself
- Providing Yourself with the Ultimate Elite Edge

"This is exactly what I have been searching for my entire life! It felt so enlightening, empowering and invigorating. I highly recommend Kirsten's work." Eddie, Vancouver

Join the Power Now Program

Over the course of eight weeks you will learn skills to help you:

1. Control Your Mind with Self-Hypnosis
2. Gain Clarity and Focus on what You Want
3. Boost Your Luck and Change Your Mindset
4. Discover Past Limiting Programming and Reprogram Your Mind

5. Release Current Negative Conditioning
6. Uninstall Unhealthy Patterns and Create Habits for Success
7. Train Your Mind to Visualize and Manifest Unconsciously
8. Create Subliminal Triggers to Boost Happiness and Confidence
+ Plus, bonus material!

"Kirsten helped program my mind to love myself. The results really do stick with me because she gave me coping mechanisms and the results just don't go away. I would definitely say to work with her because I'm somebody who has tried many forms of therapy… You will love it." Jessica, White Rock

Reprogram your mind to get what you want. Master your mind and love your life.

Group hypnotherapy and private hypnotherapy programs are available.

Would You like Your Next Event to have a Huge Life-Transforming Impact?

Can You Imagine having Your Attendees Talking about Your Event for Weeks after it has Already Ended?

When you help your team to *feel* their best, they will *perform* their best, right?

Hire me to speak at your next event and let's make it an event to remember!

My three most popular speech topics are:
1. The Art of Getting What You Want
2. Unleash the Power of Your Subconscious Mind
3. Hypnotherapy for Self-Mastery

"Kirsten's talk was unbelievable! She knows how to fascinate the audience and present them with bite size chunks that can transform their lives. I would hire her again." Allie, office manager, Vancouver

"Tremendous! Kirsten worked with my team on a weekly basis over video conference. It was one of the best decisions I made to bring her in. I highly recommend her as a speaker and trainer." Paul, business owner, Vancouver

For all booking inquiries, please contact feelingpowerfulnow@gmail.com

For more testimonials, please visit www.feelingpowerful.com/testimonials

Thank you so much for your support.

Be sure to get access to the free goodies mentioned in this book at www.feelingpowerful.com/resources

Drop by and Say "Hi" to Me Online!

Follow me on social media. I would love to hear, how has *Power Now* changed your life for the better? I would love to hear about your transformations that occurred because of this book.

Website: www.feelingpowerful.com
Youtube: www.youtube.com/feelingpowerful
Facebook: www.facebook.com/feelingpowerful
Instagram: www.instagram.com/feeling.powerful
Email: feelingpowerfulnow@gmail.com
Use the hashtags #feelingpowerful #powernowbook

Something Wonderful is about to Happen

Acknowledgements

Thank you to the brilliant and inspirational people who shared their insight with me for this book: W. Brett Wilson, Graham Lee, Nigel Bullers, Vadim Garbuzov, Denise Flores, Jennie Rodriguez-Diaz, Hector LaMarque, Jill Earthy, Raj Brar, Lien Le, Rachel David, Bryn Kenney, Devontée, Tommy Europe, Judy Brooks, Carolyn Cross, Dr. Natha, Bob Rolls, Jan Bell-Irving, David Foster at BC Top 100 Business Event 2017, Desmond Liew, Jamal Abdourahman, Janet LePage, Connor Beaton, Ramon from Salt Wellness Centre, Carolina from Sensafloat Spa, and Dr. Lois Nahirney.

Mike Cantrell, I am so grateful and pleased to have you be a part of this. It is an honor to call you my friend.

Thank you for believing in me from the very beginning and keeping me uplifted throughout this journey: Juliet and Ted van Ruyven, and Natalie Garbuzova.

Kelley Schedewitz, thank you for always being there for me when I have needed it the most. You do more than make my hair look good; you make my soul feel good. I am grateful to you and Jodi.

And the biggest thanks goes to Raf. You saved my life. And then you pushed me to write this book. I love you more than words can ever express and I am so grateful we have each other. Thank you for your love and support. Happy Life.

References

[1] Placebo- Hypertension: J Am Soc Hypertens. 2016 Dec;10(12):917-929. doi: 10.1016/j.jash.2016.10.009. Epub 2016 Nov 5.
[2] Placebo- The Power of The Placebo Effect: Newman, Tim: *Medical News Today*. MediLexicon, Intl., 7 Sep. 2017. Web. 7 Feb. 2019. <https://www.medicalnewstoday.com/articles/306437.php>
[3] Placebos without Deception: A Randomized Controlled Trial in Irritable Bowel Syndrome: Ted J. Kaptchuk, Elizabeth Friedlander, John M. Kelley, M. Norma Sanchez, Efi Kokkotou, Joyce P. Singer, Magda Kowalczykowski, Franklin G. Miller, Irving Kirsch, Anthony J. Lembo: Published: December 22, 2010.
[4] David Foster: BCBusiness Top 100 Event: 2017